W9-BMU-048

Billie Holiday

SINGER

Black Americans of Achievement

LEGACY EDITION

Muhammad Ali

Maya Angelou

Louis Armstrong

Josephine Baker

George Washington Carver

Ray Charles

Johnnie Cochran

Bill Cosby

Frederick Douglass

W.E.B. Du Bois

Jamie Foxx

Aretha Franklin

Marcus Garvey

Savion Glover

Alex Haley

Jimi Hendrix

Gregory Hines

Billie Holiday

Langston Hughes

Jesse Jackson

Magic Johnson

Scott Joplin

Coretta Scott King

Martin Luther King Jr.

Spike Lee

Malcolm X

Bob Marley

Thurgood Marshall

Eddie Murphy

Barack Obama

Jesse Owens

Rosa Parks

Colin Powell

Condoleezza Rice

Paul Robeson

Chris Rock

Al Sharpton

Will Smith

Clarence Thomas

Sojourner Truth

Harriet Tubman

Nat Turner

Madam C.J. Walker

Booker T. Washington

Oprah Winfrey

Stevie Wonder

Tiger Woods

Black Americans of Achievement

LEGACY EDITION

Billie Holiday

SINGER

Forrest Cole

CHELSEA HOUSE
An Infobase Learning Company

Billie Holiday

Copyright © 2011 by Infobase Learning

All rights reserved. No part of this book may be reproduced or utilized in any form or by any means, electronic or mechanical, including photocopying, recording, or by any information storage or retrieval systems, without permission in writing from the publisher. For information, contact:

Chelsea House
An imprint of Infobase Learning
132 West 31st Street
New York, NY 10001

Library of Congress Cataloging-in-Publication Data

Cole, Forrest.
Billie Holiday : singer / by Forrest Cole.
    p.   cm. — (Black Americans of achievement, legacy edition)
Includes bibliographical references and index.
ISBN 978-1-60413-832-0 (hardcover)
1. Holiday, Billie, 1915–1959. 2. Singers—United States—Biography. I. Title. II. Series.
ML420.H58C65 2011
782.42165092—dc22   [B]   2010026885

Chelsea House books are available at special discounts when purchased in bulk quantities for businesses, associations, institutions, or sales promotions. Please call our Special Sales Department in New York at (212) 967-8800 or (800) 322-8755.

You can find Chelsea House on the World Wide Web at http://www.chelseahouse.com.

Text design by Keith Trego
Cover design by Keith Trego
Composition by Keith Trego
Cover printed by Bang Printing, Brainerd, MN
Book printed and bound by Bang Printing, Brainerd, MN
Date printed: January 2011
Printed in the United States of America

10 9 8 7 6 5 4 3 2 1

This book is printed on acid-free paper.

All links and Web addresses were checked and verified to be correct at the time of publication. Because of the dynamic nature of the Web, some addresses and links may have changed since publication and may no longer be valid.

Contents

The Allure of Billie Holiday

Smoke hovers in the air. The notes of the last song still linger, when the club is overcome by a rare silence. The clinking of glass and ice falls silent as, by orders of the owner, the waiters stop delivering drinks to the tables and the bartenders discontinue serving them. The lights darken, leaving only a spotlight on the soft-featured face of Billie Holiday. The gardenias always pinned into her hair glisten in the light, and she begins "Strange Fruit," the final song of her set:

> *Southern trees bear strange fruit,*
> *Blood on the leaves and blood at the root,*
> *Black bodies swinging in the southern breeze,*

The imagery of the lyrics resonates with the audience, and the growing silence becomes more profound. In her soft, emotion-filled voice, Holiday continues:

Strange fruit hanging from the poplar trees.
Pastoral scene of the gallant South,
The bulging eyes and the twisted mouth,
Scent of magnolias, sweet and fresh,
Then the sudden smell of burning flesh.

It has been a few weeks since Billie Holiday began to sing "Strange Fruit" at Café Society, in New York City, but until this moment, the power of the song had yet to translate into her delivery. Suddenly the power of the song envelops her as she finishes, tears streaking down her face:

Here is fruit for the crows to pluck,
For the rain to gather, for the wind to suck,
For the sun to rot, for the trees to drop,
Here is a strange and bitter crop.

When the song is done, the lights go out completely, leaving the audience in total darkness just long enough to allow the impact of the song and the performance to set in. After an awkward moment, they burst into applause that is at once ecstatic, sentimental, and overwhelmed with emotion. It is this performance that sets the precedent for how Billie Holiday would continue to perform this song—always at the end of each set, beginning in silence, with only the singer bathed in a spotlight. Without fail, each time tears streak her face. For the remainder of her life, and afterward, this song belonged to her.

When Holiday first sang "Strange Fruit" in 1939, racism was rampant throughout the country. Lynchings like the one described in the song were still practiced with frightening regularity in the South. In the decades before the civil rights movement began in the 1950s, Holiday was no stranger to the wrath of racism. During her young life she experienced many difficulties due to the color of her skin. While the poignancy of this song scared her at first, it soon became the most important part of her repertoire. Today, it is considered one of the first songs to protest racial injustice.

Café Society, opened by Barney Josephson the previous year, was the first club in New York that integrated musicians as well as audience members, black and white. Everyone mingled freely, which was a rare occasion in those days. One day, soon after the opening, a poet and schoolteacher named Abel Meeropol (who wrote under the pen name Lewis Allan), approached Josephson and floor manager Robert Gordon with a poem that he wanted to see turned into a song. They immediately recommended that he show it to Holiday.

Allan sat down with her that night and went over the lines of the poem, carefully explaining the imagery. When she completely understood the power and meaning of the poem, she was frightened by it. A savvy singer who knew how to please a crowd, she did not believe that an audience would want to hear about such tragic events, so she told Allan that she would have to consider it. Before the end of the evening, however, she told fellow musician Frankie Newton, "Some guy's brought me a hell of a damn song that I'm going to do."

With music written by Arthur Herzog, Holiday and the club band played the song, but the first performances did not have much of an impact on the audience. As he told Linda Kuehl, who before her death amassed a large catalog of interviews with people who knew Billie Holiday, Barney Josephson could not pinpoint the exact night, but it all changed when she finally allowed the context of the song to take hold of her. (Much of Donald Clarke's biography *Billie Holiday: Wishing on the Moon* relies on Kuehl's interviews.) When it happened, though, it caused a stir of emotions that affected the audience like never before. Sadness was not the only emotion the song invoked, and there are stories about people walking out, breaking down in anger, begging her to never sing the song again, or in one case at the Apollo, the "collective sigh of 2,000 people."

The American vocalist Billie Holiday was an enormous influence on jazz and pop singing. Greatly inspired by jazz instrumentalists like trumpeter Louis Armstrong, her distinct vocal style pioneered a new way of controlling tempo and phrasing.

"STRANGE FRUIT" BECOMES IMMORTAL

From that point on, the song never failed to bring Billie Holiday to tears and take the audience for a painful visual journey through the injustices of racism. Just as the imagery had scared the singer, it scared others. Some of those frightened by the potential reaction to "Strange Fruit" were the executives at her record label, Columbia, who refused to record the song. They were not, however, opposed to it being recorded in general, so they gave their star permission to go elsewhere. She found a sympathetic ear in Milt Gabler, who owned the small label Commodore Records.

Gabler and Holiday were granted permission to record three other tunes as well, bringing the total to four songs, enough for A-sides and B-sides for two singles. In 1939, backed by her band from Café Society—Freddie Newton on trumpet, Kenneth Hollon and Stanley Payne on tenor saxophone, Tab Smith on alto saxophone, Sonny White on piano, Jimmy McLin on guitar, John Williams on bass, and Eddie Dougherty on drums—they completed the first single with a blues song "Fine and Mellow" written by Holiday, and on the flipside "Strange Fruit." The second single was "Yesterdays" and "I Gotta Right to Sing the Blues." The first single became a hit, which some accredit to the jukebox popularity of "Fine and Mellow," but the impact of "Strange Fruit" was undeniable, and soon other record companies were contacting Gabler in hopes of obtaining the rights to the song. Gabler intuitively copyrighted the

IN HER OWN WORDS...

During a live television broadcast in 1957, Billie Holiday described the different kinds of blues: "There's two kinds of blues—there's happy blues and sad blues. . . . I don't know, the blues is sort of a mixed-up thing, you just have to feel it. Anything I—I *do* sing, it's part of my life."

words and music in Holiday's name, thus securing her owner-ship of the song. Though she did not write "Strange Fruit," she claimed it as her song throughout her life, and though she would have denied it, it established her as one of the early civil rights pioneers.

2

Birth and Childhood

As a pregnant teenager, Billie Holiday's mother, Sadie Fagan, left Baltimore for Philadelphia, where she had accepted a "transportation job"—a term used for when wealthy white employers contracted African-American and other minority domestics from other, most often southern, regions. Though it was a racist method of employment, the relationship could be mutually beneficial for employer and employee, as the pay was better than the servants would receive in their hometowns and the employers were able to pay cheaper wages than if they hired someone from the city. The reasons Sadie left Baltimore are unclear, but it is known that the Fagans, her father's side of the family, were a major factor in her departure. Their critical eye and disapproval of her were no secret, and it only got worse when she announced her pregnancy, especially since the father of the child, Clarence Holiday, was also a teenager.

On April 7, 1915, at the Philadelphia General Hospital, Sadie gave birth to her daughter Eleanora Fagan. At the time of the birth, Clarence and Sadie were estranged, and on the birth certificate the father is listed as Frank DeViese. While the facts are unclear as to what relationship existed between Sadie and DeViese, to Sadie there was never any question that her daughter's father was Clarence Holiday, whom she continued to try and win back. Only Sadie knew why she put down DeViese's name, but this substitution can be seen as an early harbinger of the mixed-up life of Eleanora Fagan, soon to be known as Billie Holiday.

Soon after Eleanora's birth, Sadie returned to Baltimore, where they lived in an impoverished neighborhood in the derelict eastern side of the city. The Fagan family, except for Sadie's father, Charlie Fagan, had remained in east Baltimore. Her father's house was run by Charlie's sister Rose, a tough and unforgiving matron, who was also the driving force behind the negative family opinion of Sadie. Though Charlie loved his daughter and new granddaughter, he did not often have the courage to stand up to his sister. Why this was remains uncertain, but it has been suggested that this disapproval of Sadie was a result of the fact that Charlie had a different father from his siblings. Due to the lightness of his skin, it was suspected that his father was white. In turn, Eleanora received the same treatment as her mother from the Fagans.

After returning to Baltimore, Sadie accepted a series of transportation jobs and was forced to leave Eleanora in the care of the Fagan family. Again there is speculation about Sadie's actions. Some suggest that she took these jobs with the implicit intent of following Clarence, as she hoped to reconcile with him and bring together her little family. Clarence, however, never had an interest in being with Sadie again and was more interested in pursuing a career in music. As a teenager, Clarence had worked odd jobs in order to pay for music lessons; he had begun with the banjo, eventually moving on to

The young girl who would become the great Billie Holiday grew up on the rough-and-tumble streets of Baltimore, Maryland in the 1920s. Seen here, a period view of Charles Street in Baltimore, looking north from Baltimore Street. The city's Washington Monument is shown in the foreground.

the guitar. By the time he settled in Philadelphia, sometime after Sadie and Eleanora had returned to Baltimore, he began to play with local jazz bands. Sadie's chances of reuniting with Clarence ended in the early 1920s when he married Helen Bouldin. After he divorced Helen, he quickly married his next and last wife, Fanny Holiday.

LIFE ON THE STREETS

Because of how she was treated by the Fagan family, Eleanora felt an outcast in her own home. Such treatment made for a difficult childhood. She viewed her family's matrons with suspicion because, even at a young age, she recognized that she and her mother were treated differently and poorly. These issues were magnified by the lack of a strong father figure, as her father was mostly absent and her grandfather deferred to his sister.

For a brief moment, this all appeared to change when Sadie, at twenty-four, married longshoreman Philip Gough. Sadie's father set her up with a home, and the stability she so often sought was in her grasp. Later in life, Billie Holiday recalled how life seemed so different then, and she had fond memories of her stepfather. Unfortunately the marriage was not to last. After three years and with no explanation, Gough abandoned the family, leaving Sadie and Eleanora to fend for themselves. Unable to pay the mortgage, Sadie handed the house back to her father and moved out.

Although the Fagan family matrons were Eleanora's guardians while Sadie was away working, they did not keep a close eye on her. Left to her own accord, Eleanora spent a great deal of time away from home and school, which lent itself to time on the streets. As a very young girl, she began to develop the street savvy that would carry through into adulthood. In the fourth grade, Eleanora was attending P.S. 104 in west Baltimore, but she played hooky with regularity. Eventually she was caught by a truant officer and sent to court, where she was deemed "a minor without proper care and guardianship." On January 5, 1925, she was sent to the House of Good Shepherd for Colored Girls.

After Eleanora's release nine months later, she and Sadie moved to Fell's Point, one of the poorest neighborhoods in Baltimore. Since Sadie continued to be a domestic, still often working out of state, Eleanora's life remained pretty much the same as before her incarceration. Her penchant for the fast life of the street carried on, and she spent much of her time around hustlers and in and out of a nearby brothel. She lived in a variety of places and with different people. For a period of time, she was left with Miss Lucy Hill, also known as Miss Lu, who was the mother of Wee Wee Hill, a potential but never solid suitor of Sadie.

During this time Sadie became friendly with Ethel Moore, who owned a brothel in the neighborhood. Some have suspected that, at an early age, Eleanora was working at the good-time house. Wee Wee Hill mentioned to Kuehl, as quoted in *Billie Holiday: Wishing on the Moon*, "She hung in there with Ethel Moore. Ethel was a hustling woman and Eleanora looked to her like she was a mother. She hung in there with Alice Dean [a prostitute] and them girls, so she had to be doing what they was doing. I guess she had to get money somehow." These associations would shape the reputation of Billie Holiday, who would come to be seen as a "fast" woman. Wee Wee continued: "She wanted fast money, fast life, that's right. I knowed one boy she used to went with: Dee Dee. . . . He liked Eleanora, but she was too fast for him. After Dee Dee she went with a hustler. People knowed it; that's what give her a bad name." Another childhood friend of Eleanora's named Pony expressed a similar view to Kuehl: "Eleanora was getting around fast. . . . Eleanora just went out and done what she felt like doing 'cause she was just don't care-ish."

Along with some of the other young girls who spent time at Ethel Moore's, Eleanora was known for luring in rich white men and taking their money. Even as a young girl, she was growing accustomed to a wealthier lifestyle, even if it was procured by nefarious means. (Because Sadie would give her daughter hand-me-downs from her rich employers, Eleanora had developed a taste for the finer things in life.) During this time Eleanora was also introduced to marijuana and caroused with prostitutes and hustlers at parties, all before she was even a teenager. For a young girl, the lack of boundaries must have been exciting as well as frightening.

Also around that time, she began to sing. "Monday was Blue Monday . . . so they used to go to the different clubs and party and ball and go around to the different houses," Pony told Kuehl, as quoted in *Billie Holiday: Wishing on the Moon.* "The best dressed hustlers used to come around the neighborhood to get Eleanora for the sing. . . . A couple of boys used to sing too . . . but Eleanora take the cake. She was the big attraction. Everybody pile in when she sing." Eleanora started to earn a few dollars for singing at a speakeasy, and soon she was hopping from club to club performing. Many of the memories from that time are sketchy, including Eleanora's, so what clubs she was performing in and in what order is uncertain, but in the Prohibition era, clubs often went without names and changed venues with regularity.

Because Eleanora appeared grown up for her age, her beauty was starting to attract attention. Pony described Eleanora:

> She was young then; all the girls was young, but she was the youngest. She was tall, shape pretty nice, and by her being so young and singing so good, different fellas liked her. . . . Eleanora used to wear [her hair] back with a ribbon 'round a bun. One time she have it in a pageboy like, and another time she have it cut in a real boyish bob with a clip in back. . . . Oh, I can tell you all the women was jealous of her.

The attention she was receiving turned violent in 1926, when a family friend named Wilbert Rich raped her. Caught mid-act by Sadie and Wee Wee as they returned from a date, Rich was arrested and eventually charged with raping a 14- to 16-year-old, even though Eleanora was then only 11. He was sentenced to just three months in prison. Eleanora, however, also was punished. Because the incident was blamed on her behavior, she was returned to the House of the Good Shepherd, where she spent the next two months.

Upon her release on February 27, 1927, Eleanora— exhausted by the trouble she could not seem to avoid in Baltimore—decided to leave for New York City, where her mother had been working as a maid. With a surprising amount of experience for one still quite young, Eleanora set out on her own without a word to her mother. When she arrived in New York, she ended up living in a brothel run by a woman named Florence Williams. It has been reported, but never verified, that Eleanora worked as a prostitute during this time. Arrested in 1929 alongside Sadie, she spent six months locked up on Welfare Island for solicitation.

3

Entering Harlem

The end of the 1920s was also the tail end of the Harlem Renaissance, an African-American cultural movement. Harlem was then a bustling neighborhood in New York City. Jazz music, a key component of the renaissance, filled the air. Jazz was in transition from ragtime and Dixieland to swing and the era of the big band. Hundreds of small jazz clubs dotted the urban landscape, yet due to Prohibition—the period from 1920 to 1933, when the manufacture, sale, and transportation of alcohol were banned in the United States—many of them were clandestinely open in the basements or backrooms of brownstones and apartment buildings.

The list of club names from the era is longer than the physical locations they occupied because of a loophole in city law—if a club was closed down, which happened often, it was not necessary for a club owner to find another location, as a name change would suffice. Some locations had nearly a dozen names over the years, as various incarnations would only be open for a few weeks. Some of the more famous clubs were the Nest, which became Dickie Wells's Shim Sham Club; Clark Monroe's Uptown House; Baron's Exclusive Club; Big John's; and the Patagonia Club, which was known as Pod and Jerry's after the owners and was later known as the Log Cabin.

Though Harlem was a predominantly African-American community, the neighborhood was not as segregated as it would become in later decades. Much of this change happened

The Early Years of Jazz

Although the roots of jazz come from European and West African music, jazz quintessentially embodies the American experience in the sense that it combined a number of cultural influences in order to become its own form. Ragtime, a prototype of jazz, began in the post-Civil War era. A combination of march and African-American rhythms, it was the most popular form of music in America from the late nineteenth century until World War I. Primarily composed for the piano, ragtime is syncopated music in that it deviates from the standard pattern of high and low beats. One of its early composers was the African American Scott Joplin, who produced some of the greatest songs of the genre and was dubbed the King of Ragtime. In fact, his tune *Maple Leaf Rag* was the first ragtime hit.

In the early years of the twentieth century, ragtime spawned its first descendant, Dixieland, which emerged out of the streets of New Orleans. It embraced the blues (a form of American music that continued to blossom alongside jazz, and in many respects could be considered a sister genre), ragtime, marches, and European—mainly French—music. Ragtime was music played by one, possibly two or three, musicians, but Dixieland opened it up and a band could have more than 10 members. The sound became more dynamic as a variety of instruments were introduced, including the trumpet, cornet, trombone, piano, clarinet, guitar, banjo, tuba, drums, and contrabass.

Benny Goodman was the first Dixieland bandleader to reach a mainstream audience. This form of jazz, which was popular from the 1910s until the 1930s, spread to other centers of music, namely Chicago and the West Coast. Although originally a gospel song, one of the most famous Dixieland tunes is "When the Saints Go Marching In."

Several couples dance to jazz music, while others relax in booths at a Harlem nightclub in this July 1934 photograph. As an amateur singer, Billie Holiday was welcomed into clubs like this one.

after Prohibition, but during it, when the downtown clubs closed early, people would head uptown to pass the remainder of the night. All kinds of people were seen in Harlem clubs, including many celebrities. Even though the downtown crowd came uptown, racism was still embedded in the cultural consciousness. For example, it was forbidden in some clubs for black musicians to mingle with the white audience. One of these clubs was the famous Cotton Club, named so because it was for whites only.

While Prohibition was oppressive for the society at large, it was also responsible in part for the vibrancy of the jazz scene in Harlem. Backroom drinking establishments played host to countless impromptu jazz sessions, where the best in the industry cut their chops, battled against each other, and further developed the sound of jazz. It was also in these behind-the-scenes sessions where musicians of all races could play together without fear or worry about breaking with protocol.

ELEANORA COMES TO HARLEM

When Eleanora had reached New York City, she was broke. She soon realized that singing might be her ticket to a better life. Back in Baltimore she had already tried her hand at singing to pleasant results, so she imagined she could do something positive with her talent. There were a few hurdles to overcome at first. She suffered from tremendous self-doubt, as well as first-night jitters, which would plague her throughout her life. Even early on, however, she did possess faith in her style of singing. She never backed down from singing certain songs or yielded to a style that others wanted.

At that time in Harlem, novice singers were welcomed into some clubs to perform, but the management did not pay them. The singers would work the room by walking from table to table, all the while singing. The patrons would place bills in the singers' hands or place them on the table. Female singers could do especially well, and some had suggestive ways of grabbing the money that would earn them even more. Mae Barnes, who worked in clubs as well, told Linda Kuehl that Eleanora did not participate in the more lurid methods:

> You'd go around to the tables—me, Billie [Eleanora], an Italian girl who wanted to pass as colored, her name was Audrey. She twisted her can and took dollars off the tables. That's the kind of club it was. Billie didn't take money off

the tables. She'd go and sing, but she wasn't a dancer; she took tips with her hand. Audrey sang risqué songs, like that; we all did it. But Billie wasn't that type.

The money they earned was not great, but it was immediate.

A NAME CHANGE

When Eleanora began to sing professionally when she was around 16 years old, she decided to drop her childhood name and changed it to Billie Halliday. She took "Billie" from her favorite actress at the time, Billie Dove, and chose "Halliday" because it resembled her father's name but was different enough so that she did not appear to be capitalizing on the fame he was garnering from his work with the Fletcher Henderson Orchestra.

Clarence Holiday, a World War I veteran, had become an accomplished guitar player, and it was the musician's itinerant lifestyle that led, at least partially, to his estrangement from Sadie and Billie. He also had a reputation as a ladies' man, which earned him the nickname "Lib Lab," a musician's term for talk or in his case, the gift of gab with the ladies. Before Billie earned any fame of her own, Clarence often refused to acknowledge that she was his daughter, mainly because it made him feel old and jeopardized his chances with wooing younger women. Often, when Clarence was in town perform-ing, Billie would show up and ask him for money. Clarence was usually receptive to providing assistance but was insistent that Billie not refer to him as her father, for he wanted nothing to stand between him and the next willing woman. (Clarence, who was still married to Fanny, was the father of two children with a white woman, Atlanta Shepherd.)

While it would be a few years before the full potential of her singing ability would be recognized, many people took notice of Billie Holiday in those early years and knew that with some growth and development she could become great.

A circa-1932 exterior view of the Cotton Club jazz nightclub in Harlem. Despite the fact that its illuminated marquee presents African-American performers like Cab Calloway and Bill "Bojangles" Robinson, the club's management generally denied admission to black patrons.

There are conflicting stories as to where she got her start, but it is known for certain that early in her career she performed at most of the clubs in Harlem, not to mention in various late-night jam sessions. Caught on tape during a 1955 recording session, she tells a story about auditioning at a Harlem club called Smalls' when she was 13 years old. After she went in and the club's owners asked her what key she was going to sing in, she replied, "I don't know man, you just play." They looked at her incredulously and kicked her out. She also tells a story in her autobiography, *Lady Sings the Blues,* about being discovered at Pod and Jerry's, where she auditioned to be a dancer but was asked to sing instead. (History shows that story not to be the case as she had already been performing. The story, though, serves as a prime example of how she was prone to exaggerate her own life—one reason among many why her autobiography, ghostwritten by William Dufty, is to be read with a bit of skepticism.)

In the beginning of her career, Billie Holiday fashioned her sound after her idol Louis Armstrong, the vocalist and trum-

Louis Armstrong

Jazz great Louis Armstrong, born on August 4, 1901, is considered among the most influential musicians of his generation. Armstrong was raised in the violent and poverty-stricken New Orleans neighborhood known as the "Battlefield." He lived with his paternal grandmother during the first years of his life, and she introduced him to music through attending church.

When he was five years old, he moved in with his mother and sister. When he was old enough, it fell upon his shoulders to help support the family. One of his early jobs was selling junk for a Jewish family, the Karnof-skys. They lent him money to buy his first instrument, a cornet. Concurrently, he began to sing with a vocal quartet that performed on street corners. But during a New Year's celebration, on the last day of 1912, Armstrong was arrested for shooting a pistol loaded with blanks into the air. As a result he was sentenced to time in the Colored Waif's Home for Boys, but it was there that he further developed his musical skills, as a member of the school's brass band.

Upon Armstrong's release, he went looking for work in the honky-tonks of New Orleans's red-light district. These gigs helped him land work on the riverboats that cruised the Mississippi, but in 1922 Armstrong was presented with the opportunity to leave the South for Chicago, where the jazz scene was booming. Armstrong left New Orleans with just the clothes on his back and a trout sandwich from his mom.

When he arrived in Chicago, he joined the Creole Jazz Band, under the direction of his mentor Joe "King" Oliver. Armstrong's talent was soon apparent, and his wife at the time, Lil Hardin, encouraged him to venture out on his

pet player whose innovative sound was changing the face of jazz. Clarence criticized his daughter then about how much she mimicked Armstrong and told her that she would never succeed by copying other musicians. In the years to come, he recanted his criticism as it became more clear that she had a sound all her own. She would always admire and look up to Armstrong, but in retrospect it is easy to see that her early derivative style was a springboard for her own innovation.

Holiday's reputation in New York City grew quickly as she got regular work, with frequent stints singing at the Nest and

own. New York City's jazz reputation was growing, so Armstrong moved there to check it out and briefly played with the Fletcher Henderson Orchestra, but he soon returned to Chicago for a residency at the Dreamland Café.

During that time Armstrong laid the tracks for what would catapult him into stardom. The sides, later dubbed the Hot Five and Hot Sevens after the bands he played with, were recorded for Okeh Records from 1925 to 1928. They marked the transition of one era of jazz into another. The Dixieland style was waning; on the way in was swing, a style that meshed with Armstrong's musical abilities because it provided more opportunity for his innovative solos. Due to Armstrong's influence, the soloist acquired a new and important role in jazz music.

Armstrong's career was long and evolving. After a number of years, he left behind the more experimental playing that had made him famous and focused more on being an entertainer. During the Swing Era, he was the leader of an ensemble, but his group was never considered one of the central characters. He later formed the All Stars, which was a small ensemble that he led for the rest of his career.

Some criticized Armstrong's move toward popular music, but his vocal pop music scored some of his greatest hits, including "Blueberry Hill," "Mack the Knife," and "Hello, Dolly!" He also starred in dozens of films over the years and became one of the most recognizable faces in the world.

In 1971, Louis Armstrong died in Corona, Queens, where he was living with his fourth wife, Lucille. Thousands attended his funeral, including many showbiz and jazz legends.

the Patagonia Club. Her name was becoming synonymous with the New York jazz scene, but she was also developing contrasting reputations for her beauty and crass behavior. By today's standards she would be considered a big woman, at times weighing more than 200 pounds (90 kilograms), but many admirers saw her as beautiful, elegant, and commanding in presence. Yet she was also known for being tough; she gambled, drank, and smoked marijuana from an early age. She was prone to cursing, which, coupled with a bad temper, lent itself to frequent physical confrontations. This wild behavior, though upsetting at times, endeared her to the members of her band. They viewed her differently from most singers because they saw her as one of them. While this could be attributed in part to her singing style and ability, in the early days it had much to do with the fact that she could be just as bad as one of the boys.

A SOFTER SIDE

Despite her toughness, Billie Holiday had a tremendous need for love and affection, which in later years would too often come by abusive means. In one of her early bands, she met and fell in love with piano player Bobby Henderson. Soon the pair became inseparable. The relationship was probably the kindest of her life. After Henderson became her accompanist, they were engaged, but the marriage was never fulfilled. The arc of that relationship is telling. Holiday had been abandoned by the father figures of her life—her grandfather, her father, and Philip Gough—and abused by other men, but when she met Bobby, a gentle and sweet man, she could not allow herself to be happy. Even Bobby saw this: "She was much more of a hip woman than I was a hip young man. And it surprised me when I knew she was sixteen years old. She didn't tell me much about her early life, but I sensed it. She had a tough time when she came up." Believing he was too good for her, she gravitated toward more abusive men after their breakup and in those later relationships kept an emotional distance to protect her vulnerability. In the same way that Sadie carried a lifelong love for Clarence, so her daughter did for Bobby. Billie Holiday would love Bobby Henderson for the rest of her life.

4

Billie Begins Her Recording Career

In 1933, Monette Moore, a well-known jazz and blues singer who became popular in the 1920s, opened Monette's Supper Club. Instead of performing there herself, she hired Billie Holiday, who was accompanied by pianist Dot Hill. The run was short, however, as the club was only open for three weeks, but in attendance every night was a young record producer, John Hammond. An Ivy League dropout who was in his early twenties, Hammond had the production of a couple of records under his belt. He would become a major figure in the history of jazz in particular and of music in general, as he not only discovered Billie Holiday and Count Basie, but much later, Bob Dylan and Bruce Springsteen. Hammond had a great ear and was immediately enthralled by Holiday. He recalled in his autobiography *John Hammond on Record*:

> She was not a blues singer, but sang popular songs in a
> manner that made them completely her own. She had an

uncanny ear, an excellent memory for lyrics, and she sang with an exquisite sense of phrasing. . . . I decided that night that she was the best jazz singer I had ever heard. . . . Night after night I went to the Yeah Man, the Hot-Cha, Pod's and Jerry's Log Cabin, the Alhambra Grill, Dickie Wells', and other Harlem speakeasies to hear Billie. . . . I brought everybody I knew to hear her. . . . There was little I could do for her immediately. No one would record her. She was unknown outside Harlem, and, indeed, a vocalist who did not play an instrument—like Armstrong—was not even considered a jazz singer. I could not forget her, but all I could do was talk and write about her.

Hammond did not "forget" Billie Holiday. After he was able to procure a deal with Columbia Records for clarinetist Benny Goodman, he was able to do the same for Holiday. So in late November 1933, she had her first recording date. No memorable sides were produced during that first session, but two weeks later, she returned to the studio and recorded four additional sides with Goodman, including "Riffing the Scotch," a tune written by Johnny Mercer. This recording was one of the first steps toward wider exposure and fame. Meanwhile, she continued to make her club appearances, including a stint at the newly renamed and decorated Pod's and Jerry's Log Cabin. She also performed at Frank Bastone's Alhambra Grill and later moved to the Hot-Cha Bar on Seventh Avenue. In late 1934, her popularity began to escalate with more recordings and regular appearances around New York—but her most celebrated recordings were yet to come.

It was at that time that fellow musicians and jazz aficionados were starting to see, or rather hear, what a natural talent Holiday possessed. As Donald Clarke wrote in his biography *Billie Holiday: Wishing on the Moon*, "Billie was the first singer who was herself a great jazz musician, as opposed to a musician who also sang." Hammond recognized her ability right from the beginning. She had a knack for remembering

An early 1940s group photograph of the American bandleader and clarinetist Benny Goodman *(seated at left)* and American record producer, musician, and music critic John Hammond *(seated, second right)*. Hammond arranged for Holiday to make her recording debut with Goodman in November 1933.

lyrics and was able to excite musicians into playing and/or rehearsing. On occasion her tactic of falling behind the beat left musicians believing she was off, but Hammond knew she was interpreting the song in her own fashion. As quoted by Donald Clarke in *Billie Holiday: Wishing on the Moon*, Johnny Guarnieri told a story about a gig at the Onyx later in Billie's career. "The first night she handed me some tattered lead sheets and said, 'Give me four bars,' I played four bars. But she didn't come in. Figuring she hadn't heard me, or just missed her cue, I started over again. Suddenly I felt a tap on the back of my head and I heard her say, 'Don't worry 'bout me—I'll be there.'" And there she was, time and time again.

THE APOLLO

As her status as a local star elevated, Holiday was primed for one of the most important litmus tests of talent during the 1930s: Amateur Night at the Apollo Theater. With two balconies and seats for 2,000 people, the Apollo was one of the grandest stages in Harlem. It also had one of the most discerning audiences and has been, for many years, a venue that could make or break a career. If one succeeds on the stage during amateur night, it is presumable that he or she can succeed just about anywhere. Despite the enormous evolution in popular music during the last half of the twentieth century, the careers of many future stars were launched at the Apollo, including two of Holiday's most respected peers: Sarah Vaughan and Ella Fitzgerald.

In late 1934, Ralph Cooper, the master of ceremonies at the Apollo, heard Holiday sing at the Hot-Cha Club and told owner Frank Schiffman, "You never heard singing so slow, so lazy, with such a drawl—it ain't the blues—I don't know what it is, but you got to hear her." On this recommendation Schiffman booked her for an appearance on November 23, 1934. She was to be accompanied by Bobby Henderson.

On the night of Holiday's Apollo premiere, she was so overcome by her ever-present opening-night stage fright that she needed coaxing to go on. Unable to take the first step onto the stage, she was pushed onstage by comedian-singer Alamo "Pigmeat" Markham, who had opened the show. He recalled the day to Kuehl:

> Billie came on right before the big band closed the show,
> 'cause that was the big attraction in those days—the big

bands. . . . I guess she was tryin' to get her energy to go on stage. She was standin' in the wings before she went on; the music comes up; she froze—she just stood there. And I give her a shove—a hard shove and I didn't intend to shove her as hard as I did, and I guess she would of fell, but she grabbed on to the mike and finally she got herself together and she started singin'.

Once Holiday settled into her songs, she relaxed and performed splendidly. The audience loved her and encouraged her to an encore, a rare occurrence at the Apollo. Schiffman was impressed as well, and he booked her for a return engagement the following April. By the time the marquee went up for her return performance, her last name had been changed from Halliday to Holiday, because she no longer believed anyone would accuse her of riding on her father's coattails.

RECORDING WITH TEDDY WILSON

Holiday's emotion-filled voice was wowing the New York audiences, but she was still relatively unknown outside the city. Hammond had helped her gain some fans in England due to his articles for the British magazine *Melody Maker*. It was her next recordings, however, that would cement her place as one of jazz's greatest singers. Accompanied by pianist and arranger Teddy Wilson, she recorded many of her most memorable tunes over the next few years. In July 1935, she recorded four tracks with Wilson and a seven-piece band composed of available musicians. The session has been said to have had the energy of a jam session, which music critics by and large believe provided the magnificence of those first sides and contributed to the young singer's relaxed attitude. As opposed to her first recordings with Hammond, this band was all black, except for a Goodman appearance. The backing band in the July session, besides Goodman and Wilson, were Roy Eldridge on trumpet, Ben Webster on tenor sax, John

In this 1944 photo, American jazz pianist and arranger Teddy Wilson *(seated)* works with conductor Phil Moore at the piano. Billie Holiday's first collaboration with Wilson helped to establish her as a major singer.

Trueheart on guitar, John Kirby on bass, and Cozy Cole on drums. Two of the four songs became hits, "I Wished on the Moon" and "What a Little Moonlight Can Do." In an interview later in life, Wilson spoke of Holiday's abilities:

> [W]e rehearsed [the songs] until she had a very good idea of them in her mind, in her ear, but there'd be no rehearsal with the musicians; there was no need for rehearsals. They were all expert improvisers. Her ear wasn't phenomenal, but she had to get a song into her ear so that she could do her own style on it. She would invent different little phrases—all great jazz singers do that, do variations on the melody, and they have to know the melody inside out in order to do that.

Another session followed later that month, but this time Wilson prepared an arrangement of songs. The imposed structure, however, versus the free flow of the first recording session, had an ill effect on Holiday. Because the restraint of the arrangements can be heard in her voice, none of these songs enjoyed any lasting popularity. Further sessions, however, were more successful, including one that produced "I Cried for You," which sold 15,000 copies, a relatively high number in the 1930s. Yet because this was an era before artist royalties, most musicians never earned a cent after the session. Though she had a hit song on her hands, Holiday did not earn a dime beyond her $50-a-session pay. In a decade or so this would all change, but during those early years she was earning a paltry amount.

After the popularity Holiday gained from the Apollo performances and the Wilson recording sessions, she knew it was time to find a manager who could help her book gigs and secure payment. She soon met Joe Glaser, a white club owner and booking agent who also managed Louis Armstrong. The relationship started with the occasional gig, but Glaser soon signed Holiday to an exclusive contract, which lasted most of her life. Although Glaser was tough, he and Holiday were able to establish a good working relationship, albeit one beset by the occasional talent/manager arguments. Throughout Holiday's life, Glaser was the first to help her out when needed, but also the first to reprimand her for bad behavior.

Glaser, who hailed from Chicago, was reported to have ties to Al Capone and other gangsters. Despite these underworld connections, he was a fair and respected manager, who, after becoming Armstrong's manager in the late 1920s, helped the already famous trumpet player secure good high-paying gigs. (In fact, one of the first gigs Glaser booked for Holiday was at Connie's Inn, where she had the opportunity to play alongside her idol.) Before working with Glaser, Armstrong had been taken advantage of by a number of managers, and though criticism of Glaser is varied, Armstrong was always grateful to him. Glaser's relationship with Holiday, on the other hand, was a roller-coaster ride. Their fights were infamous among those around at the time, and Glaser was known for his tricks, withholding money at certain times so she was

IN HER OWN WORDS...

In a 1956 interview with Willis Conover, Billie Holiday recalled the influence that Louis Armstrong had on her singing:

I think I copied my style from Louis Armstrong. Because I used to like the big volume and the big sound that Bessie Smith got when she sang. But when I was quite young, I heard a record Louis Armstrong made called the "West End Blues." And he doesn't say any words, and I thought, this is wonderful! and I liked the feeling he got from it. So I liked the feeling that Louis got and I wanted the big volume that Bessie Smith got. But I found that it didn't work with me, because I didn't have a big voice. So anyway between the two of them I sorta got Billie Holiday.

forced to continue to work with him when he knew that she was looking elsewhere. For the most part, however, Glaser watched over her, made sure she was paid, and took care of her as her health deteriorated in later years.

Meanwhile, Holiday and Wilson recorded together incessantly. On one occasion in March 1936, however, she missed a Wilson session due to another engagement and her spot was given to a young Ella Fitzgerald, who would become as much of a jazz legend as Holiday, if not more popular in the mainstream. In 1936 alone, Wilson recorded 27 songs, 13 of which were with Holiday.

At the same time, Holiday had her first solo recording session (her first session in which she was the featured singer, not just the singer for a particular band), where she joined with clarinetist and future jazz legend Artie Shaw. The session produced some quality sides, including, most notably, an impromptu blues tune dubbed "Billie's Blues," one of only two blues songs she ever recorded. American music was evolving and Billie Holiday along with it. In its next incarnation, it would take her to even greater heights.

5

Life of the Swinging Big Band

Joe Glaser sent Billie Holiday to his hometown of Chicago for a residency with the Fletcher Henderson Orchestra at the Grand Terrace, which was run by his friend Ed Fox. Trouble was almost immediate. Before Holiday was set to perform on the second night, Fox brought her into his office, where he began to criticize her singing and question her suitability for his club. Holiday never took kindly to criticism, especially from a white man, and responded vehemently, trashing his office and throwing furniture. Although Fox had a reputation as a tough guy, he met his match in Billie Holiday. Not surprisingly she was fired, and her run ended after just one performance. When Glaser showed that he was unsympathetic to her concerns about how Fox had treated her—and even suggested that she "speed up the tempo"—she replied, as she would in one form or another throughout her life, "I'm going to sing my way, you sing your way."

Upon Holiday's abrupt return from Chicago, she and her mother moved into a new apartment, which happened to be above an empty restaurant. This allowed Sadie to fulfill her desire of having her own business. She opened up a soul-food restaurant, which quickly became a hangout for musicians, many of them broke and hungry. But Sadie welcomed them all, money or not.

Even though mother and daughter had their rows, they continued to live together, and when separated, they longed for each other's company. Their relationship was dysfunctional to say the least. Holiday often treated her mother cruelly, but Sadie was known for sticking her nose in her daughter's business, which grated on her fiery independence. Sadie could be overbearing, clingy, and fragile, while Billie could be obstinate, bullish, and childish. These traits made for difficult living, not to mention that they both had issues of abandonment and rejection, having been ostracized by their larger family and left behind by Clarence. Because Sadie's history of rejection by multiple men was a heavy burden on her, she turned this into guilt, which she laid upon her daughter with tremendous effect. Many of Holiday's problems with drugs and alcohol would later be attributed to her lack of confidence, which many believed was a direct result of her difficult childhood. As Hammond saw it, "Billie wasn't terrible to her mother, but she wasn't good to anybody. Billie was horribly abused by life."

THE STREET

Back in New York City, Holiday's first engagement was at the Onyx Club on Fifty-second Street, a burgeoning center of jazz, but after three weeks she was asked to leave because of jealousy from the headlining act, a sextet fronted by Stuff Smith, who felt that she was upstaging him and taking his thunder. The owner, Joe Helbock, was indebted to Smith and the money his act had been garnering for the club, so he let Holiday go.

The Street, as that strip of Fifty-second was known, was then the center of the New York City jazz club world. It was home to such well-known clubs as the Down Beat, the Famous Door, and the Yacht Club. From the 1930s and continuing through the 1950s, anyone who was anyone in jazz played there. Not only did Billie Holiday make a name for herself there, but so did Count Basie and a number of later musicians responsible for the transition of jazz from swing to bebop, including Thelonious Monk, Charlie Parker, Dizzy Gillespie, and Miles Davis.

Though clubs existed in Harlem and elsewhere, the Street was the place to perform. It was the place Holiday knew she needed to be. After being let go from the Onyx, she found work at Clark Monroe's Uptown House for the following three months, then returned to the Street to perform regularly at all the clubs, including another engagement at the Onyx while Smith and his band were away on tour.

THE PREZ

During her tenure at the Uptown House, Holiday became friends with Lester Young, a soft-spoken but brilliant saxophone player. They met at a January 1937 recording session, where he performed on "I Must Have That Man." Never lovers but the closest of friends, they shared a similar demeanor, a liking for marijuana and drinking, and musical talent with deeply ingrained sentiment. Though their instruments were different, music critics have commended them for their ability to take each respective one beyond expectation.

Early in her career Holiday's voice was often criticized for its lack of depth and body. That her style was different, there is no question, but it was *her* style and she stuck with it, no matter the requests or demands. In time the musicians around her began to understand her approach to music. Like no other singer before her, Holiday used her voice not to carry a tune alone but as an instrument. To her backup musicians, it was not like backing up a singer, it was like playing with a fellow musician, who was improvising with the song. Yet it was not only her mastery of her voice that endeared her talent to everyone, but also her emotional commitment to the song. She invoked sympathy when she sang, and her complete surrender

DID YOU KNOW?

BILLIE AND HER DOGS

In the late 1930s or early 1940s, dogs became an important part of Billie Holiday's life. Her first dog was named Rajah Ravoy. According to Holiday, he was not the brightest of the pack, so she believed he deserved an intelligent name. After Rajah Ravoy died around 1944, Holiday was heartbroken. Then came Moochie, a gift from Lester Young, but her next dog, Mister, became her companion for many years. He posed with her in numerous pictures and accompanied her to all of her shows. He would hang out in the clubs, being cared for by everyone who knew him, but his true love was Billie. He would even wait patiently in her dressing room for her to finish singing. There were rumors, however, that Billie and some of her friends would shoot Mister up with drugs. Eventually she gave Mister to Bobby Tucker. After Mister, her next dog was a Chihuahua named Chiquita, and she later brought in another Chihuahua named Pepi. She babied Pepi, and even fed him from a bottle, which some reported could have been filled with gin.

In this circa-1945 photo, Billie Holiday sits by a window holding a record, with one of her beloved dogs lying at her feet.

spoke of empathy. Listeners truly believed that when she sang about love, loss, or both in a song, it was truly coming from her own experience.

The popularity and understanding of her delivery, however, was initially limited to musicians and critics, as the public took much longer to acclimate to her style. Lester Young suffered a similar fate. His sound was subtle, less in-your-face, than some of his peers. Like Holiday, he spent much of his career unknown to a wide audience even though fellow musicians considered him one of the best saxophonists in jazz. In fact, younger players who mimicked Young's style often were more famous and better paid than he. Because Young and Holiday had much in common and shined in each other's company, it was surprising to some that they were not an item. Those closest to them, however, insisted that theirs was strictly a platonic friendship based on respect and a shared melancholy. Lee Young, Lester's brother, told Kuehl, "If you'll listen closely, he played the way she sang, and she sang the way he played."

The duo soon had more opportunities to commiserate, after Young discovered a rat in the drawer of his hotel bureau. He subsequently moved in with Holiday and her mother, and as a result of their time together, the three were graced with nicknames that would follow each of them to the end of their lives. Early in her career, Holiday—always known for her style, beginning in her childhood when she wore the hand-me-downs from Sadie—had already garnered the name "Lady" from some of the girls with whom she worked. But the nickname "Lady" was bestowed on her originally, in part pejoratively, because some viewed her attitude as pretentious. Lester lengthened her sobriquet to "Lady Day," instantly removing any negativity by gracing her with a name suggestive of royalty. She returned the favor, dubbing Young "the President," most often shortened to "Prez." Continuing on the line of doling out names suggesting nobility, Young graced Sadie with the nickname "Duchess."

Life appeared to be moving quickly toward success. Holiday was performing regularly and continuing to record with Wilson. Then, on March 1, 1937, she received a phone call to let her know that her father had died. It has been said, but not verified, that during Clarence's tour-of-duty in World War I, he was exposed to toxic gases that severely affected his lungs, so much so that whenever he became ill it was necessary to consult a doctor immediately. (Clarke disputes this story, stating that Clarence never made it to the European theater and had actually stayed stateside during his military service.) While Clarence was on tour in Texas, he became sick, but because of segregation in the state, he waited until the tour bus reached a city before going to a hospital. Unfortunately, by the time he checked himself in, it was too late, and he succumbed to complications from pneumonia. Billie's relationship with her father was spotty and complicated. While she often visited him when he was performing in New York, his support of her singing took time. It was only after other musicians accepted her that Clarence gave his full support. Nevertheless, his loss grieved her tremendously.

COUNT BASIE

A week after her father's death, Holiday left the Uptown House and was offered a position, at $70 a week, with Count Basie's touring 13-piece orchestra, which included Lester Young on saxophone, Buck Clayton on trumpet, and blues singer Jimmy Rushing. Such a large touring ensemble would have been unusual in earlier years, but not at the beginning of the Swing Era.

John Hammond had brought Basie and his band out from Kansas City in 1936 and began to introduce them to audiences in New York. At first they were not well received, which some members of the band attributed to their collection of old and deteriorating instruments. The band had never made much money, but that soon changed after it recorded, in 1937, the hit "One O'Clock Jump." By today's standards the money was

The Swing Era

Evolution is an inevitable part of music. Jazz has gone through many changes since its inception in the late nineteenth century. After ragtime, Dixieland, and hot jazz entered swing. Continuing the syncopation of ragtime and the large ensembles of Dixieland, swing introduced a free-flowing, four-beat measure into the fold. The early changes have been accredited to Louis Armstrong and his innovative trumpet playing, when in 1924 he briefly joined the Fletcher Henderson Orchestra. As a result, his upbeat playing was introduced to a wider audience, thus bringing the swinging sound to cities across America, namely New Orleans, Chicago, Kansas City, and New York.

Throughout the 1920s swing stayed underground while Dixieland flourished, but as is the case in many of the arts, the roles were soon reversed. By the early 1930s, swing was beginning to sweep the nation. Soon ballrooms around the country were filled with big band music. Bandleaders such as Fletcher Henderson, Benny Goodman, Count Basie, Glenn Miller, and Artie Shaw commanded groups of talented musicians, some of whom would eventually lead their own bands.

Because the opening up of the tempo made swing great music to dance to, many styles of dance were created, such as the lindy hop, the jitterbug, the shag, and the jive. There were also distinct geographical forms of dancing broken up into West Coast and East Coast swing. For roughly 10 years, from 1935 to 1945, swing was king of popular music in America and around the world. And, for the only time in American history, jazz was the most-listened-to genre of music: Swing made jazz mainstream music.

Although the instruments involved in swing were very similar to Dixieland, including the clarinet, trumpet, guitar, trombone, piano, drums, and saxophone, one significant difference was that the double bass replaced the tuba. The structure of a swing band was based on orchestrated pieces punctuated by solos that expanded upon the melody. During these solos the individual musicians had the opportunity to showcase their talent. Although such solos were a time for innovation, there were limits—each soloist was bound by adherence to the general melody. To some musicians, that structure became stifling, and soon the wheels of evolution began to turn, as musicians broke away from the big band and formed smaller ensembles, from which bebop was born.

Swing, however, would experience a resurgence in the 1990s with such modern bands as the Cherry Poppin' Daddies, Squirrel Nut Zippers, and Big Bad Voodoo Daddy.

still a pittance as royalties had yet to be introduced, but the record helped introduce Basie to Holiday. Basie was instantly impressed with the young singer, and when she joined the band, he knew she would create a much-needed dynamic. Basie spoke with Kuehl:

> Musically, there was a great change, *great* change made in the band. Something added, a wonderful attraction that we had. Everybody loved her, everybody got along with her; she got along with all the guys, and that was something else that was wonderful. . . . Playing for her was just too much. . . . Billie was a musician. That's the way the guys felt about Billie.

Again Holiday was able to blend right in with the boys, and she endeared herself to her bandmates. She was not only admired for her musical abilities, but also for her willingness to gamble, curse, and drink with the best of them. For the first time since Bobby Henderson, she fell in love with a fellow musician, guitarist Freddie Green, who was married with two children. She states, somewhat vaguely, in her autobiography, "It was the first time I was ever wooed, courted, chased after. He made me feel like a woman. He was patient and loving; he knew what I was scared about, and he knew how to smooth my fears away." She never mentions Green by name, but the timing is right for this reference to have been about him.

After Holiday made her debut with the Count Basie Orchestra in Scranton, Pennsylvania, they returned to New York for dates at the Apollo and the Savoy Ballroom. Afterward the band went back on the road, eventually touring the South, where traveling with an all-black band was difficult. It was often hard for members to find places to stay, especially together as they often preferred. If they found a house big enough for them all, they would pile in, cook together, and rehearse for the upcoming shows.

In this circa-1945 photo, American jazz guitarist Freddie Green plays an acoustic guitar in a recording studio. Green was one of the great loves of Billie Holiday's life.

In early 1938, the Count Basie Orchestra returned to New York for a concert at Carnegie Hall. After an appearance at the Apollo, however, Holiday was fired from the band. Her strong-willed nature, though respected by her peers, conflicted with the management team that had financed the tour. They cited her unreliable performances as the reason for her firing. Such complaints became more persistent throughout her career. Holiday worked according to her own terms. If people had a problem with her style of singing, then it remained, according to her, their problem. After the press blamed Hammond for the firing, studio executive Willard Alexander stated in a press release, "The reason for her dismissal was strictly one of deportment, which was unsatisfactory, and a distinctly wrong attitude towards her work. Billie sang fine when she felt like it. We just couldn't count on her for consistent performance."

Another problem area that persisted and affected people's perception of Holiday's professionalism was her punctuality and occasional disappearances before important performances. In response, she remained defiant. She believed that, if she did not feel like performing well, no one could wrestle it out of her. Such an attitude proved to be a double-edged sword: It was as responsible for her status as an innovator as it was for her selfishness, which was often upsetting to those who depended on her.

Although music critics have long praised Holiday's performances with the Count Basie Orchestra, due to contractual commitments to Brunswick Records, they never recorded together in a studio. There are, however, a few live recordings so fans can enjoy the sounds of Billie Holiday and the Count Basie Orchestra, most notably the album *At the Savoy Ballroom*.

THE ARTIE SHAW ORCHESTRA

Not much time passed before Holiday found more work with another touring band, the Artie Shaw Orchestra, in March 1938. The band had not been together long when she joined, and again she introduced an interesting dynamic. As they were already on tour, she joined them in Boston, much to the joy of the band. Bassist Sid Weiss remarked, "Billie sang coming in and out of the different parts of the program. That was one of the high points. I'm sorry no one ever recorded it." Unfortunately, just as had happened with Basie, she was unable to record with Shaw, who had been on the Brunswick label but had recently switched to RCA. There is only one recording of Holiday with the orchestra, on "Any Old Time"—likely her only studio recording with a big band. During that same session in July 1938 (but without Holiday), Shaw recorded "Begin the Beguine," which not only went on to become a hit but is now considered one of the top songs of the Swing Era.

An all-white band with a black singer posed many problems. At the time racism was rampant throughout most of the United States, but it was especially prevalent in the South. Shaw was an ardent opponent of racism and did everything in his power to help assuage the situation for Holiday. No matter his efforts, however, there were times when nothing could be done. There were also plenty of times when he was unable to fully grasp his singer's plight of being considered, simply due to skin color, a second-class citizen. This was especially disheartening to Holiday, as white club patrons would pay for and enjoy her singing, but then insult her with derogatory and racist language.

One date in the South turned sour when Holiday was forced to stay in the outskirts of town at a black hotel because she was barred from staying in the same hotel as the band. Then in St. Louis, a promoter who was afraid of the audience's reaction, demanded that a white singer replace her. Although Shaw stood up for her at first, he later succumbed to pressure and hired Helen Forrest, who stayed on with the band for just such future occasions.

Holiday was at first understanding of the situation and welcomed Forrest, but she grew exponentially upset when the new white singer began to get more and more appearances. Though racism appeared to her to be at the root of those problems, executives at the record company and club management argued that the change had more to do with Holiday's style of singing, which they said was not traditional enough.

The final straw and the incident that ended Holiday's tenure with the Artie Shaw Orchestra happened in New York. She expected racism down South, but not at home. For an engagement at the Lincoln Hotel, in late October 1938, the owner insisted that she enter the venue via the kitchen. He also expected her to remain sequestered in a room between sets, while the rest of the band was allowed to patronize the hotel bar. Such treatment infuriated her. When Shaw sided with the owner, she felt betrayed. She was also forced out of the twice-weekly radio broadcasts set up by Columbia because the program's sponsor, Old Gold cigarettes, did not want to put a black singer on the air. Again, Forrest was brought in to replace her on those occasions. By December she gave her two-week notice and swore never to work for a big band again. While the Artie Shaw Orchestra went on to great success, pulling in $25,000 a week and producing hit after hit, Billie Holiday was about to embark on a significant new phase of her career.

6

The War Years

After Billie Holiday's experiences on the road with the big bands, the intimate setting of the clubs in New York City appeared safe, comfortable, and a respite from the harsh realities of life during the mid-twentieth century, including economic upheaval, racism, and the threat of world war. In such smoky, booze-filled clubs, she felt at home and performed with aplomb and confidence. Longer runs in clubs also helped her cope with her first-night jitters. On the road, first nights happened with more frequency, but at a club, once a residency was under way, she could adjust, regain her confidence, and move forward without anxiety.

Upon Holiday's return to the city, a new club opened in the West Village. Satirically dubbed Café Society and owned by Barney Josephson, the club seated 220 people under its motto: "The Wrong Place for the Right People." Josephson had been a shoe salesman when he borrowed money from friends to finance his dream of creating an egalitarian venue for jazz. Although many of the jazz clubs of Harlem during Prohibition had catered to a mixed audience, the United States was still beset by racism, leaving many clubs divided by race. Holiday and her fellow black musicians experienced such segregation on a daily basis; they often performed in clubs where they were prohibited from mingling with or speaking to white customers. This treatment had especially infuriated Holiday, who often tried to stand up against these injustices. While she would never have claimed to be a revolutionary, a dissident, or a politico in the struggle for civil rights, she was never one to hold her tongue when she knew she was being mistreated.

In December 1938, when Josephson opened the doors of the new club, it was an integrated venue where black and white audience members and musicians mingled without restriction. A new era in jazz was born. Café Society and its policy revolutionized the club scene and opened the eyes of many a visitor—and Holiday found a perfect setting for her style of performance and attitude. After Holiday performed on opening night accompanied by Sonny White, Café Society became her home for the next nine months. In an interview from the late 1980s, Josephson spoke of those times:

> Billie was my first female singer, when I opened Café Society in the winter of '38. She was the star of the show I had, working with Jack Gilford, who was the MC and comic and just starting in show business. I had a band led by Frankie Newton. . . . Billy Kyle was his pianist and Billie's accompanist. With Big Joe Turner, and boogie-woogie pianists. John Hammond helped set it up.

Besides performing, Holiday was also continuing to record some tracks with Teddy Wilson, some with other musicians, and the occasional solo recording. While many of these songs were popular and some were hits, she was not introduced to

Billie Holiday performs with her signature flower in her hair at the Offbeat
Club, in Chicago, Illinois, in 1939. As World War II was gearing up in
Europe, Holiday was coming into her own as a singer and recorded one
of her most famous songs, "Strange Fruit," at this time.

the most poignant song in her repertoire until her residency at Café Society. Poet and schoolteacher Lewis Allan wrote the words to "Strange Fruit," a moving and graphic anti-lynching poem. His search for a singer to interpret and translate his words into song landed him at Café Society.

Holiday doubted her ability to deliver a song with such poignancy, even though many have claimed that her greatest gift as a singer was her ability to become one with the song and its meaning. With "Strange Fruit," though, she was uncertain of her ability to sing the song the way it deserved. Her trepidation was short-lived, however, and she decided she was ready for the challenge.

"Strange Fruit" changed Billie Holiday's career. While this early protest song opened the doors for similar songs in the

Racism and American Jazz

Even though the American Civil War had freed millions of slaves, a negative result of this change was a magnified resentment of African Americans. In the South especially, such overt racism could be vicious and deadly. After the Civil War, the Ku Klux Klan, a white supremacist group, saw an increase in membership, and segregationist Jim Crow laws created highly restricted lives for African Americans. Racism often boiled over into vigilante justice. One method of vigilante justice favored by whites in the South was lynching. This practice was widespread well into the 1930s, when Billie Holiday was first introduced to "Strange Fruit."

Violence in the South, coupled with a lack of economic opportunities, forced many African Americans to the urban centers of the North. As a result, places like Kansas City, New York, Boston, Chicago, and Philadelphia became hubs of music development. The southern city of New Orleans appeared to be a partial exception. It was not without segregation or racism, but the French- and European-influenced cosmopolitan environment was a hotbed for creativity and was moving much more quickly toward integration.

As the predecessors of jazz were emerging, it was difficult for African-American entertainers to find equal footing. Many black musicians at the time could not secure gigs outside of "their" communities, and those who

future, the subject matter allowed Holiday to add dramatic intent and palpable emotion to her performances, which further endeared her to many. Even though lynching was still widely practiced in the South, and the pictures of that time are graphic and powerful, the images were not widely circulated. In her own way, Holiday brought such tragedies to the forefront of people's consciousness. And once the song was part of her regular schedule, it became the one with which she would end each evening.

Following Holiday's first run at Café Society, and with the recent success of her recordings, she began to receive top billing and earn good money for her appearances. This newfound fame was exciting for her, but it also caused problems—now club owners, who had sold tickets to patrons on the guarantee

did were few and far between. Even when someone experienced mainstream fame, the compensation was always less than that of white musicians. Scott Joplin, "The King of Ragtime," was one of the first African-American jazz composers and performers to reach a wide, not just black, audience. Nonetheless it was a slow crawl toward any measure of equality.

Even after jazz became the most popular form of American music in the 1930s and 1940s, racism was still a troubling issue, especially in the South. Black musicians were forced to stay in separate hotels, were told not to mingle with the audience, and were often forced to stay backstage between sets. Such treatment was not only experienced in the South, but also in plenty of other cities. It was not until the integrated Café Society opened in the late 1930s that a club existed without racial boundaries.

Significant change did not begin to take place in the United States until the civil rights movement started in the 1950s, and in many ways, jazz was at the forefront of integration. Even though musicians were segregated by race, behind closed doors, in jam sessions and backstage, black and white musicians mixed and played together with regularity. Music brought the races together and was responsible in part for planting some of the seeds of the civil rights movement.

One of Billie Holiday's most enduring songs is "God Bless the Child," which she cowrote and recorded in 1941. It was also one of her last hit singles.

that she would perform, demanded her punctuality. Her lack thereof, in the past, could be overlooked or forgiven because Holiday was not the headliner; a no-show now produced not only profound disappointment among fans, but it also meant club owners took a hit at the box office.

After the "Strange Fruit" session, Holiday was back in the studio frequently and on a few dates recorded with the same personnel that backed her at Café Society. She also recorded with members of Basie's band, including Lester Young. Some of the songs she recorded in those months were "Some Other Spring," "Our Love Is Different," "Them There Eyes," "The Man I Love," and "You're Just a No Account." The last number includes a solo by Young.

In June 1940, she was back in the studio again with Wilson. The lineup for these sessions was strong and included, among others, Roy Eldridge on trumpet, Freddie Green on guitar, and Young on tenor sax. The sides included a song attributed to Holiday, "Tell Me More," though according to songwriter Arthur Herzog, he cowrote it with Daniel Mendelsohn. While he never had enough proof to make the change in the song-writing credits, he demonstrated in interviews that he did not hold any resentment.

In May 1941, Holiday recorded "God Bless the Child," which was one of her last hit records. The song, inspired by her mother, was written by her and Herzog. As Herzog recalled to Kuehl, Holiday told him: "That's what we used to say—your mother's got money, your father's got money . . . but if you haven't got it yourself, God bless the child that's got its own." Even though Herzog and Mendelsohn had put most of the song together, they gave half the songwriting credit to Holiday.

Although "God Bless the Child" was a breakthrough for Holiday, she still struggled to reach a wider audience. This was especially true of white audiences, who were often looking for someone more traditional, someone perhaps more comfort-able to their ears. While she was a jazz singer, Holiday had also become a pop singer—in fact she could be considered the first pop singer because she had helped jazz move from its instru-ment-centric leanings to a style based mainly on the vocalist.

That said, Holiday, who was singing popular songs of the day, was nonetheless struggling to get the attention she so desired. Ella Fitzgerald, on the other hand, burst onto the scene and was able to garner almost all the attention from the charts, audiences, and critics. When critics compare the two, Holiday is often considered to be more innovative and a better interpreter, for her voice was like an instrument unto herself, but Fitzgerald had the more powerful voice that could attract the masses. While Holiday would remain a cult favorite, she never broke into the mainstream. This deeply affected her, and coupled with her stage fright, rebellious attitude, and growing dependency on drugs and alcohol, her reliability faltered.

UNRELIABILITY ESCALATES

When Holiday did not show for the opening night of her second run at Café Society, Josephson, who was enjoying plenty of success with other acts, immediately canceled her contract. However, there was no lack of venues wanting her to perform. She could easily find a job, but her reputation for being unpredictable was growing, making it hard for her to find long-term work. She hopped from venue to venue, and city to city, performing for a variety of audiences. Though she was never in one place for very long, she was recognized more and more as a phenomenal jazz singer. Unfortunately, this was also at a time when she was gaining notoriety for bad behavior.

One area of her life in which Holiday often self-destructed was in her relationships with men. Though she had known some decent ones like Freddie Green and Bobby Henderson, for the most part, she walked away from those relationships because they were too good to be true and quickly fell back to dating abusive men, who were often reminiscent of the pimps she was around at such a young age. In 1941, while performing at the Famous Door, she became reacquainted with Jimmy Monroe, the brother of the club's owner, Clark Monroe. Their romance was quick and fiery; within months, on August 25, 1941, they were married, much to the disappointment of those closest to Holiday, including her mother and Joe Glaser.

There are numerous accounts from people who knew her who claim that Holiday, who often had an innocent demeanor, welcomed the abuse. Later in life, some claimed that she appeared to push her men to the brink and wanted them to beat her. On multiple occasions she had to cancel performances due to black eyes and a swollen face, but some of those same accounts relate how she would emerge from her dressing room after a brawl with her man at the time happier and ready to perform. Whatever truth was behind her behavior or those statements will never be known, but in retrospect it is apparent that she chose men she thought could protect and provide for her, but who were also abusive and manipulative. Her marriage to Monroe was the first in a line of detrimental relationships.

The pull of the fast life continued to be a strong influence on Holiday, who gravitated toward those who could provide such a lifestyle. She was already known for her drinking and gambling, as well as her penchant for smoking marijuana. Josephson, who did not allow drugs in his club, said that she used to leave between sets and smoke marijuana in a cab while it drove around. In the beginning, the drug use appeared to be her attempt to numb her stage fright and boost her confidence; it was not until later that she was introduced to hard drugs by Monroe, who had a heavy opium, and possible heroin, habit.

Because of Sadie's disapproval of Monroe, Holiday moved out of their home for the first time since coming to New York. Soon afterward, the couple left for her first appearances on the West Coast. She began a run at Café Society, in Los Angeles, which had no connection to the East Coast club and, in fact, was soon sued by Josephson and forced to close. When the West Coast Café Society closed its doors, she was left broke and needed to borrow money to get home.

Even though her prospects, opportunities, and recording and appearance fees were growing, she always lived beyond her means, no matter how much money she made.

Monroe, hoping to earn some money, decided to stay on the West Coast, which basically ended their marriage. She tried numerous times to reconcile with Monroe. This led to no avail, however, and left her brokenhearted and addicted to hard drugs. What had started as her adding bits of opium to her coffee led to a much larger problem.

Following the breakdown of her marriage, Holiday continued to hop from club to club, playing venues all over the East Coast and Chicago. In May 1942, she returned to the West Coast and played two months, with Lester Young, at Billy Berg's Trouville Club in West Hollywood. The scene in Los Angeles excited her because she was able to rub elbows with so many movie stars, including Orson Welles, Humphrey Bogart, Tallulah Bankhead, and Clark Gable. Such intimate encounters always left her beaming.

At the end of her run at the Trouville Club, Holiday recorded for Capitol Records one of her less-regarded but often performed songs, "Traveling Light," written by Trummy Young. According to Holiday's autobiography, when she and Trummy Young recorded the song, they had been struggling financially—they were making money, but they also had a hard time not spending it. They hoped that the $75 apiece they would earn from the recording session would be enough to get them back to New York, but once they had the money in their hands, they decided to celebrate and ended up blowing it all in one night. Holiday was forced to borrow money to get home, this time spending days on a cross-country bus—not the most elegant mode of travel for a rising star.

Upon her return to New York, she commenced a long residency at the Onyx. During that engagement she met Joe Springer, who would become her accompanist for the following two years. After their run at the Onyx, the duo moved to the Yacht Club, but Holiday's troubles with commitment and a fixed schedule arose again, leaving her searching for another place to sing, one where the management did not mind her unreliability. (She also worked on and off, for five years, at another Street establishment, Kelly's Stable.)

Being reliable was not easy, as Holiday loved to keep her own schedule. If she wanted to go hang with the boys instead of doing a show, she believed that was her prerogative. One place she liked to frequent was Minton's Playhouse in Harlem. An all-star cast of musicians performed there, including Roy Eldridge, Dizzy Gillespie, and Kenny Clarke. One of the regulars was a 25-year-old trumpet player, Joe Guy. She most likely knew Guy from other clubs, but Minton's was where they first hit it off—although it is likely that their attraction could also be attributed to their mutual addiction to heroin.

Holiday vehemently defended all her boyfriends against the accusation that they were responsible for her addiction, but she did later admit that her serious habit did not begin until she was married to Monroe and that she had started taking drugs in as a way to reconcile their marriage. Guy, however, had a habit that would pull Holiday deeper into her own addiction. Her reliance on drugs only exacerbated her trouble with punctuality.

IN HER OWN WORDS...

In her autobiography, Billie Holiday did not shy away from her experiences with drug addiction. She wrote, "If you think dope is for kicks and for thrills, you're out of your mind. There are more kicks to be had in a good case of paralytic polio or by living in an iron lung. If you think you need stuff to play music or sing, you're crazy. It can fix you so you can't play nothing or sing nothing."

HEROIN

When discussing Holiday's drug use in the early years, namely the 1930s, most of her friends stressed that she was not taking anything harder than marijuana or alcohol. This changed in the early 1940s, when she began to use heroin heavily. The effect heroin had on her became more noticeable. In August 1944, during a residency at the Down Beat Club in New York, reviewers commented on her dramatic weight loss and stark appearance—the drugs were obviously taking a toll on her body. She also missed dates at numerous clubs in New York and had a number of contracts canceled. At Clark Monroe's Spotlight Club, she missed opening night, but Monroe forgave her and she went on to a spectacular residency.

Bebop

As fans of swing were bouncing around the ballrooms in the late 1930s, some young jazz musicians were listening intently to the sounds of their predecessors, such as Lester Young and Coleman Hawkins. It was not the organized sounds of swing that attracted them, but rather the excitement and improvisation of the solo. Musicians like Young and Hawkins not only used the solo to expand upon the melody of the tune being played by the rest of the band, but they also used that opportunity to offer their own individual take on jazz. Young and Hawkins both played the tenor saxophone, but Hawkins's delivery was robust and aggressive, while Young's was soft and mellow.

Beginning in the early 1940s, these successors to Young and Hawkins developed a new type of jazz, one that was strikingly different from swing. Bebop, or bop as it is often called, was born from the solo, and though it still relied on the ensemble structure, the bands were much smaller than those associated with swing. The number of band members was cut from 10 to 16 down to 4 to 6, which allotted more time for experimentation and improvisation from each member. Most significantly, bop migrated away from the easily danceable tunes that had made swing so famous and widespread. The tempo picked up speed, the beats at times became irregular, the melodies became complex, and more and more the players gravitated away from

Guy and Holiday decided to put together a 16-piece touring band, but neither of them was aware of the financial drain associated with an endeavor of this magnitude. It cost them nearly $35,000 just to set things up, and without proper discipline, it was difficult to get the musicians organized, making the task of loading everyone on the bus quite hard. These troubles continued as they moved through the South. Adding to their struggles was the changing face of jazz. As the big band era was nearing its end, a new style of innovative and improvisational jazz emerged, dubbed bebop.

During a tour stop in Washington, D.C., Holiday learned that her mother, Sadie, had died. She was 49 years old. Holiday was left distraught by the news and claimed to have

composition. Jazz evolved—or devolved according to some—from music that was great to dance to into music that was great to listen to. To some, bebop was classified as art music, and in turn it became more academic than swing, Dixieland, or ragtime.

Most historians and scholars concur that the name "bebop" stems from scat singing, a form of improvisational nonsense singing, which grew more popular concurrently with bop even though it had been around since the early twentieth century. "Bebop" was one of the nonsense words often repeated.

Two early pioneers of bebop were Dizzy Gillespie and Charlie Parker. Gillespie, a jazz trumpet player, played with a number of big bands during the 1930s, including those run by Cab Calloway, Ella Fitzgerald, and Fletcher Henderson, but his penchant for experimentation isolated him from many of his fellow musicians and at times infuriated the band leaders who wanted the ensemble to stick to the prescribed composition.

While Gillespie lived into the 1990s and watched jazz evolve many times over, Parker—like so many others of that generation—was addicted to heroin and died in 1955, but not before he made significant contributions to jazz and bebop. His alto saxophone tunes and improvisations on the alto saxophone are considered some of the most influential of the period. Other significant bebop musicians were Thelonious Monk, Miles Davis, and John Coltrane.

7

Addiction and Decline

In late 1945, Billie Holiday returned to New York City to play a stint at the Down Beat Club. The following February, she had her first solo concert, at Town Hall, where she was accompanied by Joe Guy, Joe Springer, Tiny Grimes on guitar, Lloyd Trotman on bass, and Eddie Nicholson on drums. Promoted by Greer Johnson, the Town Hall concert was structured unlike any other jazz concert that had preceeded it, in that it was more like a recital of classical music. About it, Robert Coleman said, "In a sense, it is a jazz lieder program and not a jam session." To Linda Kuehl, Johnson described the work that went into getting his star performer ready for the show:

> I had to get Billie up a full hour-and-a-half before, get her dressed, which wasn't easy, come downtown through the mob scene that had grown outside Town Hall—and on the way down, Billie suddenly decided she wanted another

dress, that she wanted to wear a second dress for the second half. . . . By the time we got to the hall I was hysterical, but she still went on on time.

The performance, however, was an enormous success. Reviews lauded Holiday's presence and delivery. She sang 18 songs and was in very high spirits, most likely due to the audience's response. Her confidence always soared when the response was positive, unlike instances in clubs when she believed patrons were not giving her the attention she deserved, which could affect her mood for days or push her toward leaving the stage, not to return.

THE DECCA YEARS AND "LOVER MAN"

A couple of years earlier, in 1944, Columbia Records, claiming to not like the changes Holiday was making in her singing style, did not sign her to another contract. She moved to Decca on a one-year contract. One of the first releases was "Lover Man," a song that included strings, a rare addition in jazz, and was arranged and directed by Salvador Tutti "Toots" Camarata. The song went on to become the equivalent of a top-20 hit—her last song to reach that high on the charts. As a result her contract with Decca was extended. Though she did not produce more hit records for the label, her sales were still high, making her a valuable asset to Decca. In those first few years, she recorded a number of notable songs, including one of her own, "Don't Explain."

In September 1946, Holiday went to Hollywood to realize her lifelong dream of appearing in the movies. She would appear alongside Louis Armstrong in the film *New Orleans*, which was dubbed "the story of the odyssey of jazz." The film starred Arturo de Córdova and Dorothy Patrick, plus a number of other jazz greats including Kid Ory, Meade Lux Lewis, Red Norvo, and the Woody Herman Orchestra. Unfortunately, both Armstrong and Holiday played stereotypical roles for

African Americans; she appeared as a singing maid. Holiday, who normally grew quite upset by such treatment, was relatively casual about the experience, telling Leonard Feather, "I'll be playing a maid, but she's a really cute maid."

During filming Holiday came into conflict with the film's star Dorothy Patrick. She writes in her autobiography, "After the 'star' looked at a few days' rushes she decided I was stealing scenes from her." Punctuality became a problem as Holiday was also working club dates while on the West Coast, but it was rumored that the union workers did not mind her tardiness because it guaranteed them overtime pay.

Critics panned the film, with the exception of the performances by Holiday and Armstrong. Although the film portrayed such overt negative stereotypes, all of the reviews but one refused to touch upon this sensitive issue. The one standout was by Holiday's friend Leonard Feather, who wrote in *Metronome*:

> Socially, Mr. Levey [the producer] bent over backwards to avoid offending the South. Billie Holiday is (of course) a maid, Louis Armstrong talks to his horn, no Negro shakes hands with a white man, and the cast racial overtones of the story are carefully muted. . . . [U]ntil Hollywood stops pussyfooting on the race question, and makes a picture with the attitude that it doesn't give a damn whether the South shows it or not, there will not be any real movie about jazz.

After the experience of *New Orleans*, Holiday vowed never to work on another film, but despite the negative reviews and stereotyping of the film, it did have one positive outcome for her—a further introduction to a much-wider audience.

When she returned to a residency at the Down Beat, she found herself without an accompanist one day. Pianist Bobby Tucker, who happened to be walking by, was hailed off the street by his friend and fellow musician, Tony Scott. The show

From left, Louis Armstrong, Billie Holiday, and Barney Bigard perform on the set of the film musical *New Orleans* in 1947. Holiday's experiences in Hollywood did not enamor her to the then-segregated world of filmmaking, though her performance in the film did impress many movie critics.

was set to start in 10 minutes, and a full house awaited. Tucker agreed and became Holiday's regular accompanist for the next few years, until 1949. Years later, Tucker discussed Holiday's method of singing with Kuehl, "Wherever I put the tune, she found the groove and made it happen. She could swing in the hardest tempo and float on top of it like it was made for her; when I put it slow, she sang it slow—but the most beautiful slow you ever heard."

BUSTED

Around this time Holiday, at the behest of manager Joe Glaser, checked herself into a New York clinic to undergo a "cure" for her heroin addiction. Her unreliability was becoming a detriment, and some clubs were insisting that her pay be docked if she did not show. Glaser hoped that persuading her to check into the clinic would not only help her overcome her heroin problem but would also show club owners that she was trying to fix her problems with punctuality. This supposed cure was a cold-turkey treatment, which consisted of flushing her veins with glucose. Such a method was in no way able to cure an addict, because it did not treat the cause of addiction but rather just eliminated the drugs from the body. The mental dependence on the drug still existed within her; all the purification did was make it so she was once again susceptible to the full potency of the drugs. (Most addicts, when in the thick of their addiction, are just taking drugs to feel normal.) As Tucker said, "All it does is make her a virgin when she comes out."

Yet the cold-turkey remedy appeared to work at first. Upon her release, she moved to the house of Bobby Tucker's mother in New Jersey. This foray helped prevent the inevitable for a brief spell—as soon as she was back on the music scene, her habit returned.

Holiday tried to keep her stay at the clinic a secret, as she did not want the authorities to be aware of her drug use, but inevitably word spread. Due to the press she received during her cure, she was immediately put on the watch lists of the Federal Bureau of Investigation (FBI) and local authorities. It was not long before they came after her. She had been previously caught by an FBI agent named Jimmy Fletcher, who had found her in possession of a syringe and a quarter of an ounce of solution. The case was too small to pursue, since no real drugs had been found, but because of her high-profile life, the police were eager for a bust. Fletcher later told Kuehl that Glaser was partially responsible for the authorities' attention on Holiday, as he desperately wanted to see her kick both her habit and Joe Guy to the curb.

In May 1947, Holiday shared a bill with Louis Armstrong at the Royale Theater in Philadelphia. After the final night, she returned to the hotel to collect her things. Her road manager Jimmy Ascendio and Tucker were already there. When she approached the hotel, she realized that a bust was taking place and, according to one account, she ordered her chauffeur to flee the scene and return to New York. The chauffeur, afraid because he had previous arrests, fled in a panic and hit another car. The crash attracted the attention of the police, who began to fire at the fleeing vehicle. There are, however, varying accounts of this story, including one that has Holiday driving away at high speed under a hail of bullets, but they are unverifiable. It should be noted, however, that, according to Agent Fletcher, he inspected Holiday's car and found it riddled with bullets.

Even though authorities in New York, New Jersey, and Pennsylvania had been alerted to her fugitive status, Holiday and her driver managed to make it back to New York City without incident. She met up with Guy, who had also avoided being arrested in Philadelphia, and they got a room at the Grampion Hotel. She went about her business as usual, going to clubs and performing, and all the while Agent Fletcher followed her. Glaser hoped she would turn herself in and tried to persuade her to do so by saying that the worst that could happen was that she would be forced into another treatment. But before she could do so, her room at the Grampion was raided, and she and Guy were arrested for possession of heroin.

While out on bail, Holiday abided by Glaser's request and returned to Philadelphia, hoping for a quick and lenient trial. Such was not the case, however, as she was found guilty of heroin possession and sentenced to a year and a day in the Federal

Reformatory for Women in Alderson, West Virginia. (In true Billie fashion, as the great defender of her abusive men, when called to appear for the prosecution during Guy's trial, she flipped and helped to set him free.) Her time in prison was reported as serene, and she spent a good amount of it working and cooking for the prison and the prisoners. She was released after nine and a half months, on March 16, 1948.

CABARET CARD PROBLEMS

Upon her release, Holiday took the train to the Tucker house in New Jersey, planning on a smooth transition back into the New York scene. Before she even reached the house, though, she fell back into old habits, much to the dismay of Tucker, as she had bought heroin during a train change in Washington and showed up at the house high. Despite her state, she and Tucker got down to business staging her comeback. As she had not sung a note since being incarcerated, she worried about being able to sing at all, but immediately upon her arrival, Tucker began to play the piano and she fell back into her groove without trouble.

Though her voice was intact, Holiday found her return to New York to be quite difficult, because at the time it was illegal for anyone with a felony conviction to have a cabaret license. This meant that she was barred from performing in any club in the city. She could, however, perform at theaters. In March 1948, she had her welcome-home concert at Carnegie Hall. The show was eye-opening for Holiday: People cared for her, which was something important with her low self-esteem. With this adulation fueling her, she performed remarkably. Tucker described it to Kuehl:

> It was fantastic. It was unbelievable. There were seats in
> the aisles, and there were about six hundred people sitting
> on the stage. Nowadays that's against every fire law in New
> York. The musicians—and there were only four—had to

On March 27, 1948, Billie Holiday played to a sold-out crowd in Carnegie Hall in New York City. The concert marked the beginning of her comeback after her arrest and imprisonment a year earlier on narcotics charges.

carry their instruments above the crowd to get on stage. There were people sitting around the piano, and it was like a living room. Everybody was scared to death until the introduction to the first tune. It never was a contest; it was just pure fun.

The concert set a new box office record for Carnegie Hall. Holiday sang 21 songs, and the audience called her back to the stage for six encores. The reviews and turnout were so impressive, she was immediately booked for a return engagement three weeks later, which broke the box office record she had previously set.

Despite this triumph, it became increasingly difficult for Holiday to find work, due to the cabaret license problem. Those who were able to book her, however, always did great. She was packing houses in record-breaking fashion, but some of the allure might have been because of her status as a junkie and a felon. She was well aware of this phenomenon and was often distraught that some people came to her shows to see her mess up or messed up.

A NEW LOVER

A small reprieve came when Holiday met John H. Levy, the owner of the Ebony Club and a reported gangster, who for unknown reasons was able to circumvent the law. Whether he had cops on the payroll was unclear, but the law did not bother her at the Ebony. This not only helped her financially, but impressed her emotionally. Soon, Levy and Holiday were a couple. Her relationship with Levy was not much different from her previous ones, but one difference was that Levy did spend his *own* money on her, buying her fancy clothes, jewelry, and a car, and helping to set her up in an apartment, but he used this as a way to control her life. Their relationship, like so many of the others, was fueled by passion that often turned to abuse. Many times she was spotted with black eyes and a bruised face. Though she was often a victim, she could dish out a sound beating as well—there are numerous accounts of her physically besting men when they offended her. At times she assaulted Levy.

Levy and Holiday seemed to feed off this crazy energy; at times, instead of beating on each other, they teamed up against others. One such occasion happened on New Year's Eve in 1948 at Billy Berg's in West Hollywood. Holiday was two weeks into a residency at the club, and after her performance that night, she was hanging out in the kitchen. What led to the fracas is unclear, but Levy was witnessed entering the kitchen, and it appears he became jealous or enraged by another man's behavior toward her. He grabbed a butcher knife, and while Holiday was throwing bottles, he stabbed an onlooker in the shoulder. He very well could have been going to stab the intended target intentionally, but the man who ended up with a knife in him was someone on the sidelines of the ruckus. Holiday and Levy were arrested and charged with assault with a deadly weapon, which put the singer in the headlines once again.

Because of her return to a more rounded physique, it seemed that she was no longer using heroin. Then, in January 1949, during a residency in San Francisco, she and Levy were arrested for possession of opium. After their hotel room was raided, she was caught trying to flush the drugs and paraphernalia down the toilet. She claimed that Levy asked her to hold the drugs, and rumors followed that Levy was responsible for the bust. Holiday claimed to not be using drugs at the time, and she consulted a friend, Dr. James Hamilton, who checked her into a clinic for observation. During that brief stay Dr. Hamilton did not see any symptoms of withdrawal, and Holiday was able to use this evidence to convince the court of her sobriety.

Having tired of northern California, Holiday traveled to Los Angeles to perform at the Million Dollar Theater. Although the arrest did not lead to a conviction, she left behind several upset people, including her lawyer for the case and two club owners, who demanded that she owed them money. These claims led to lawsuits. Much of the debt was due to Levy, who had control of her finances and had refused to pay the bills, instead keeping the money for himself.

His behavior continued, and Holiday insisted on defending him. Her support did not last, however, when, in 1950, Levy promised to act as guarantor for her band's salary, but the band was left foraging for funds. One reason the band was not making any money was because Levy had failed to promote the tour, and when they entered the South, the situation became dire. Levy came and went but never left any money to support the band, and finally it reached a point where they could not continue. The trombone player Melba Liston told Kuehl:

> We were at a hotel, and we checked out, and the bus driver hadn't gotten his money; they didn't pay him and he stranded us in South Carolina, and we spent a few nights on the bus waitin' for him to come back. She and John [Levy] pulled out with the promise to send money back for us . . . while we were on the bus it was terrible. The cops used to come by every night with the sticks and threaten us that if anything went wrong in town the guys were responsible, and we got frightened, and I was going to pieces until I got out of there.

The money never arrived, and the band was forced to find its way out of the South. Levy's refusal to pay for the band affected Holiday, and he no longer had her support. After this debacle she split from him for good.

8

The Final Years

By the middle of 1949, Bobby Tucker, who had grown tired of John Levy's behavior and mistreatment, moved on, leaving Holiday once again looking for an accompanist. She continued to hop from one coast to the other, trying to outrun the trouble that appeared waiting around every corner. There is no denying that much of this drama was self-created. Upon a return to California, the narcotics bureau once again came looking for a bust. That time, however, Holiday was not around and her chauffeur was arrested for possession of two packets of heroin. If the drugs belonged to Holiday, it will never be known because the driver said nothing and was subsequently handed a prison sentence.

Holiday was a difficult person to gauge. There were moments when she would be effusive with praise and love and others when she could treat an old friend with a mysterious coldness. This happened years later when the chauffeur was released from prison. When he showed up at the club where Holiday was singing, she refused to even say hello to him. Many have suspected that her erratic behavior was influenced by the drugs, but Holiday, on drugs or off, had always been a fickle and temperamental lady.

In the meantime Holiday found another accompanist, Carl Drinkard. After California she headed back east, stopping in Chicago for a residency where she was surprisingly lauded for her punctuality as well as for her performances. Then she returned to Philadelphia, where she reunited with Lester Young, but bad luck in that city continued to plague her. For unclear reasons, she and Young had a falling-out, which lasted nearly three and a half years. Some have speculated that the split centered on the hypersensitivity of both Holiday and Lester, coupled with their insecurity, but none of that is certain, as it has also been reported that Lester was fed up with Holiday's heroin use.

Because of her inconsistent behavior and reputation for drug abuse, Holiday was not re-signed to Decca in 1951, but she accepted a yearlong contract with Aladdin Records. Not only did she change labels but she also found a new beau in Louis McKay, while working at Club Juana in Detroit. They had been friends some years earlier but were reacquainted in a quick romance, which soon led to marriage. McKay also became Holiday's manager and adviser. Holiday flipped coasts again, at McKay's request, so that she could earn club wages and work on paying off the debts she had accrued during the last debacle in California. In March 1952, her contract with Aladdin expired, and Holiday moved to the Mercury label, which was then run by Norman Granz. She was also primed to go on a European tour later that year, but it was canceled at the last minute when one of the headlining acts was forced to stay in the United States because of delinquent tax payments.

BEBOP REIGNS SUPREME

In the 1950s, the jazz scene had changed. Bebop, which had begun in the 1940s, was in full bloom, even entering its second generation. The big bands had gone out of business, and bebop was the new thriving style of jazz. To keep working, Holiday had moved from jazz to pop. Even though she preferred the older style of jazz, the new influence could not be ignored. With stars like Miles Davis, Thelonious Monk, Charlie Parker, and Dizzy Gillespie at the forefront of the bop movement, the demographics had been altered. The Street was changing, and clubs were closing. Some of the scene moved back uptown to Harlem, some of it went downtown to the West Village, some moved elsewhere throughout the country, while others went to Europe, where black musicians, especially famous ones like Louis Armstrong, were treated much more fairly.

Other changes were afoot during that period, namely the introduction of television, which enjoyed a post-World War II influx into the American home. Holiday was able to broaden her audience by appearing on the occasional broadcast, including a 1952 appearance on Duke Ellington's *25th Anniversary in the Music Business Concert* at Carnegie Hall. The show was a great success, and her performance was considered one of the highlights, among an all-star lineup that included Stan Getz and Miles Davis. Her inability to play clubs continued to affect her, but Holiday was still able to access New York audiences through the theater circuit, where she performed to sold-out crowds.

Then, in 1953, a show about her life, *The Comeback Story*, was aired on a coast-to-coast broadcast. It told her story in detail, complete with some of the turmoil of her early years and a frank discussion about her dependence on heroin. Her fellow musicians and friends were asked to appear on the show, but many were reluctant, which was evidence of a growing concern about associating with Holiday. The show was a success, however, and a sufficient number of performers appeared alongside Holiday.

A photo of Billie Holiday performing in concert in 1954, the year she first visited Europe as part of a package concert tour that also included American jazz clarinet player Buddy DeFranco and American jazz vibraphonist Red Norvo.

EUROPEAN TOUR

In 1954, Holiday finally got her wish to perform in Europe, but it was almost curtailed again because she did not have a birth certificate, which was needed for a passport. She was, however, able to find a baptismal certificate, and with an added letter from the Mother Superior of Baltimore's Sacred Heart Chapel, she was granted a passport.

Organized by Leonard Feather, the package tour of Europe, dubbed "Jazz Club U.S.A.," featured Holiday, accompanied by Drinkard, as the headliner. The other acts on the tour were Red Norvo's trio, Buddy DeFranco's quintet, and Beryl Booker's trio.

On January 9, 1954, they left New York for Europe. The tour began in Scandinavia, with the first date in Stockholm, Sweden. Unable to fly directly there, they landed in Copenhagen, Denmark, and boarded a train to take them the remainder of the way. After 11 hours of travel, they arrived with only a short time remaining before the concert. Exhausted and jet-lagged, the musicians struggled through the first couple of shows.

After the shows in Sweden, the tour played Denmark, and then Norway. The musicians began to settle in, and the energy and morale of the tour improved. They moved on to Germany, Switzerland, and France. After three weeks the package tour came to an end, but Holiday and Drinkard went on to England for additional shows. (The other acts were prohibited from joining them due to conflict with a music union in Great Britain.)

Holiday's popularity in Europe, especially in England, had always been great. For nearly 20 years, she had been trying to cross the Atlantic to meet her fans. At the gate she was met by a throng of journalists, including Max Jones, who was a huge fan of Holiday's and became a lifelong friend. When she first

IN HER OWN WORDS...

In her autobiography, Billie Holiday described her approach to singing, particularly when she was on tour and performing the same songs each night: "I can't stand to sing the same song the same way two nights in succession, let alone two years or ten years. If you can, then it ain't music, it's close-order drill or exercise or yodeling or something, not music."

arrived in Britain, many of the questions at a press conference centered on the more dramatic aspects of her life, namely her lack of a cabaret card and how that affected her work in New York City. After she began to perform in the United Kingdom, however, the press turned its attention to her performances, beginning at the Free Trade Hall, in Manchester.

Her final performance of the short tour was at the famous Royal Albert Hall, in London, where she was backed by Jack Parnell's Band. For 6,000 people, she played 15 songs and encored with "Strange Fruit." Though it was reported that Holiday stormed out of her dressing room after the show in tears, she had nothing but high regard for the experience and the audience, often commenting about how different the reception was in Europe. Even before leaving England, she expressed her desire to return. She stayed for a while longer and performed at the Flamingo Club, in the Soho neighborhood of London.

After her return from Europe, Holiday was back to her regular routine, still contesting the absence of her cabaret card. She fired Drinkard. They had had a good working and personal relationship, but since he was an addict as well, it made for difficult times. She continued to record for Granz, and then was asked by him to perform at the Jazz at the Philharmonic concert at Carnegie Hall. Already on the bill was Ella Fitzgerald, but he believed the stage was big enough for these two lady dynamos of jazz. During the first set, Holiday performed with aplomb and was received with much regard. In between the first and second set, Holiday returned to the dressing room. When she came back out onstage, she was a mess and unable to keep the beat. At the end, Granz had to help her off the stage. It is likely that between sets she had gotten high.

The next major concert was more of a triumph. In the summer of 1954, Holiday was asked to perform at the inaugural Newport Jazz Festival. Playing on Sunday night, she was one of the showcases of the event, and a special band was put together for the occasion. Teddy Wilson, after many years, once again accompanied her on piano, and the rest of the quintet was composed of solid and true players: Jo Jones on drums, Milt Hinton on bass, Buck Clayton on trumpet, and Gerry Mulligan on baritone sax. The night proved to be even more special when Lester Young walked onstage after the first song and joined Holiday and the band for the remainder of the set. The Prez and Lady Day had not spoken in three and a half years, and the reconciliation came where their friendship began, with music. After the concert, Holiday and Young embraced and all was forgiven.

Although the small club was still the proving ground for jazz musicians, large concerts, like the Newport Jazz Festival, were becoming more commonplace. And since Holiday was limited to playing clubs outside New York, concerts like this one were her lifeblood.

After the reunion with Young, Holiday joined him on an all-star package tour, which included the Count Basie Orchestra, Sarah Vaughan, and Charlie Parker and the Modern Jazz Quartet. The tour began at Carnegie Hall, and the schedule was hectic. Holiday had a new accompanist by then, Memry Midgett, who told a story to Linda Kuehl about Holiday burning the candle at all ends. Midgett was not fond of McKay and believed that he manipulated Holiday, often forcing her to abide his wishes even when she had a pressing engagement. On one such occasion McKay had Holiday, who most likely offered, cooking for a large group of his relatives in the hours before a show. Midgett showed up and had to drag her away, get her ready along the way, and bring her to the stage. The crowd waited in anticipation as Holiday listened for the notes that would identify the song. She did not hear them. Basie, believing she might be overpowered by the big-band arrangement, had Midgett just play the opening chords. Even then Holiday could not determine what song she was supposed to sing. Finally Holiday identified the song, and she burst into her set. The crowd was wowed by her performance despite the rough beginning and encouraged her to sing encore after encore.

HEROIN'S TOLL

The impact of Holiday's heroin addiction was obvious to many for years, but it was around that time that the visual effects of her drug and alcohol habits became readily apparent to all. At normal weight, Holiday tipped the scales at just over 200 pounds (90.7 kg), but because of her habit, she had lost 85 pounds (38.5 kg) and was looking frail and emaciated. Her arms were covered in track marks from needle use, and the skin on her face was taut and had lost its suppleness. Despite these problems, her natural talent could not be denied, and she performed some fantastic and memorable shows, but only when she was able and willing. Her busy schedule coupled with her fast living made certain performances quite poor, and when the management rubbed her the wrong way, there was no chance to get her to perform well.

In 1956, Philadelphia proved once again to be a difficult place for Holiday, when she and McKay were arrested in their hotel room for possession of narcotics. She claimed to be clean at the time and stated that the stash belonged to McKay, who had asked her to hold it. The case would eventually be dismissed, but the constant trouble surrounding Holiday began to leave her ostracized from those around her, making her more and more lonely. Her self-confidence was never high, but a state of melancholy overtook her. Her depression added to the drama in her life. Also at that time evidence of McKay's ever-growing domestic abuse became more apparent as Holiday had to cancel shows, including a date at the Apollo, because her face was too swollen and bruised to appear onstage.

LADY SINGS THE BLUES

Following the arrest in Philadelphia, Holiday's autobiography, *Lady Sings the Blues*, was published to mixed reviews.

Ghostwritten by journalist William Dufty, the book describes Holiday's early struggles, arrests, prostitution, and singing career. While the book is very frank about many aspects of Holiday's life, many facts have since been refuted and proved incorrect. Plus in later interviews, Holiday—who was known for embellishing her past to ensure a good story—claimed to have never read the book.

Though the book revealed what appeared to be Holiday's darkest secrets, it also brought her new heights of popularity. Her shows were consistently sold out. Everywhere she performed, she could demand the highest of fees because it was practically guaranteed that the club or theater would be booked solid—that is, if she showed up. She continued to city-hop, playing in Detroit, Baltimore, and back in Philadelphia, where she met Mal Waldron, who was to be her final accompanist.

In 1957, Holiday not only split with Granz but she also moved to Columbia Records. After her last California residency, McKay decided to stay and settle there. Once Holiday moved back to New York, the couple officially split by the end of the year. With McKay gone, she felt lonely and depressed and spent much of her time alone in her apartment on Eighty-seventh Street near Central Park.

It is not known if Holiday was still using heroin at this time as she claims to have been clean. What was clear to those who knew her then was her increasing dependence on alcohol. Before shows she would need to drink in order to sing, and she would show up to recording sessions with two bottles of booze and a pack of mixers. At that point she was drinking two fifths of hard liquor a day. Her mood swings grew worse, and the slightest thing would send her into a fury. She lashed out at her closest friends and burned many bridges.

Another European tour was planned for 1958. Holiday was excited to return to a place where she felt comfortable and welcome, but the Algerian War forced the temporary closure

The cover of the paperback edition of Billie Holiday's autobiography, *Lady Sings the Blues*, coauthored with William Dufty. Holiday disowned the book almost as soon as it was printed.

On December 8, 1957, Billie Holiday performs with musicians *(from left)* Lester Young, Coleman Hawkins, and Gerry Mulligan in New York City on the CBS television program *The Seven Lively Arts*.

of French clubs where most of her tour was to take place, so the entire trip was scrapped. Once again the European theater escaped her.

Holiday's health was quickly deteriorating, but she continued to sing in theaters and on television. The national exposure brought her crisis to the attention of a much wider audience. Soon the press began to speculate about the cause and eventual outcome. That was a tough time for Holiday. She could demand top dollar for performances, but the work was inconsistent due to her failing health, and if she was not up to performing, then club owners knew the show would be a disappointment. With this inconsistency Holiday was, at times, forced to ask for financial help from her friends.

In the late summer and early fall of 1958, Holiday went to California for a series of shows. It was there that a doctor diagnosed her with cirrhosis of the liver. While on the West Coast, Holiday was asked to perform on the final night of the Monterey Jazz Festival. It was reported that she partially succumbed to her reoccurring first-night stage fright. According to some, she appeared nervous and timid, but the audience did not notice and responded with enough applause to encourage three encores.

Soon afterward Holiday's dream to return to Europe was fulfilled, but it began on an inauspicious note. During a performance in Milan, Italy, she was booed and hissed off the stage. Holiday, always sensitive to audience reaction, was especially dismayed, though she chalked it up, rather casually, to the language barrier. The club's owners canceled the contract after only one night. Friend and admirer Mario Fatoria, however, stepped in and provided Holiday with a unique experience, singing in the opera house La Scala, where he hosted an invitation-only performance for friends and dignitaries in Milan.

After the disappointment in Italy, Holiday traveled to Paris, France, where she performed at the Olympia Theater. The reviews were mixed, but for the following residency at the Mars Club, the performances were solid. The money was paltry compared to what she normally made, but she was happy to be performing in Europe. When no other well-paying gigs surfaced, though, Holiday returned to the United States. During the winter of 1959, Holiday returned again to Europe, but only for a few days, as she went to England to appear on the television program *Chelsea at Nine*.

Going to Europe had always been a goal for Holiday, especially England, where some of her earliest and biggest fans lived. Life there appeared better to her. Racism was less prevalent, at least in the music business, and on the few occasions she visited, she was treated like royalty. Holiday was quite ill during that quick trip in the beginning of 1959, and her appearance on television made her English audience even more aware of her condition.

By March, Holiday was back in New York, and that month Lester Young went into cardiac arrest and died in his hotel room. The doctor's statement read that his condition was quickened by alcoholism. Despite the reconciliation between Lady Day and the Prez, their friendship had never been the same. That melancholy duo could not find a way to get past their mutual sadness and reunite completely. They did, however, keep in contact via a mutual friend, and Holiday was most certainly saddened by Young's death. She and many legendary musicians attended the funeral services.

Holiday's life was mimicking that of Young's in many ways, and her own alcoholism continued to take a toll on her health. By the spring of 1959, she could no longer work regularly and only took gigs when she was feeling up to it. This was not much different from her mind-set of earlier years, but to be limited physically rather than through attitude forced Holiday onto a roller-coaster ride of the spirit. At times she was up, and during others the sickness was obvious to everyone. On her forty-fourth birthday, Holiday threw a party at her apartment, where she appeared in good spirits, but her physical appearance terrified everyone there. Many of them insisted that she go to the hospital. Ever resistant to being told what to do, Holiday refused. To show everyone how wrong they were, she completed a successful week at the Storyville Club in Boston, and some present were amazed at her return to temporary glory.

HOSPITALIZATION

When she returned to New York, she performed at the Phoenix Theater in Greenwich Village, which was to be her final show. Afterward she needed to be assisted home, and the following day, Joe Glaser and Leonard Feather came to her apartment to once again try to persuade her to check into a hospital. Again she refused. For a short while she was under the care of her personal doctor, but on May 31, she fell into a coma and was rushed to Knickerbocker Hospital. Because of the track marks in her skin, the doctors and nurses assumed her coma was due to an overdose, and she was sent to Metropolitan Hospital in Harlem, where she was left on a gurney in the hallway until her doctor found her and demanded better treatment.

The doctors at the hospital still assumed that the coma was connected to an overdose, but over the following days, Holiday showed no signs of withdrawal. This suggests that, at the end of her life, she had finally given up heroin, but no one knows for how long. Once conscious, Holiday received a long line of visitors, including Louis McKay, who flew out from California. The attention lifted her mood, and an optimistic spirit was quite visible. She even began multiple negotiations with folks for new autobiographical articles and a possible film.

The optimism of the moment was soon quashed when, on June 12, the police raided her hospital room and discovered a small packet of heroin. The details of the raid are a bit murky: Many claim it was a setup by the police, while others say someone had left the heroin behind, believing it would help comfort Holiday in her final days. According to some sources, the location of the heroin was too far from Holiday for her to reach in her condition. This did not matter to the police who, though they could not move her from her bed, posted a 24-hour guard outside her room. They took away all of her amenities and left her feeling disgraced and lonely. A friend and lawyer, who was appalled by this treatment, drafted a scathing letter condemning the police for their actions upon such a sick woman. He was able to persuade the powers that be to remove the constant police presence and return her personal belongings.

Holiday's attitude was as positive as possible, all things considered. She continued to talk about the future and was making deals for movies, books, and articles to be made after she was released from the hospital. That, however, was not to happen and she fell more ill. Her last rites were read to her on July 15, and two days later, according to William Dufty, at just past three in the morning, "her face relaxed," and she died.

Holiday's funeral took place at St. Paul the Apostle, a Roman Catholic church in New York City. Many friends and fans attended the funeral, totaling around 2,500 people. There were plans to have her buried in a plot upstate, but McKay demanded that she be buried in the same place as Sadie, at St. Raymond's Cemetery in the Bronx.

Influence and Legend

Billie Holiday's enormous influence on jazz and later forms of music remains unchallenged. Until her ascendancy, jazz had focused on the instrumentals; singers would come in only with a refrain or a short verse, often for just seconds of a song. But Holiday's unique vocalizing and empathetic delivery changed the role of the singer in music. Her voice became one of the instruments. Soon roles were reversed throughout jazz music, and the focus shifted to singing. Vocals carried the song, and the instrumentals became a backdrop. In a way, pop music as we now know it was born through the work of Billie Holiday.

Contemporary singers can give thanks to Holiday for helping move this role to the forefront of music. Frank Sinatra told *Ebony* in 1958: "With few exceptions, every major pop singer in the U.S. during her generation has been touched in some way by her genius. It is Billie Holiday who was, and still remains, the greatest single musical influence on me. Lady Day

A 1957 photo of Billie Holiday. Although mainstream success eluded her in life, Holiday was deeply respected by her fellow musicians, including admirers like Frank Sinatra, for her intimate approach to singing.

is unquestionably the most important influence on American popular singing in the last twenty years." Though music has changed immensely in the years since Sinatra spoke those words—and it may be hard for a contemporary listener to directly hear Billie Holiday's influence on modern music—it is clear that without her, things surely would have evolved differently. Besides Sinatra, singers who were influenced by Holiday include Ella Fitzgerald, Sarah Vaughan, Dinah Washington, Peggy Lee, Dick Haymes, and Perry Como. Biographer John Chilton summed it up: "Her singing has guided dozens of lesser artists into vocal stardom, and to this day, she is named as an influence by almost everyone who shapes words and lyrics in the art of jazz vocalising."

It may be surprising that someone held in such high regard never produced a hit record during her lifetime—or posthumously for that matter, as collections of her work continue to be produced. That said, her songs have continued to amass money from royalties, something Holiday did not much benefit from during her lifetime. Shortly before her death, however, she had begun to receive a considerable amount of money for each record sold. The year after her death, her royalties were upward of $100,000. According to the law, McKay was the rightful heir to her fortune. Though separated, they had never divorced, so he and his children became the executors of her estate. As a result there has been drama over her estate. There are those who support McKay and his claims that, even though they were separated, he had been there for her right before and during her final days. Others suspicious of McKay have claimed that he was just out for the money and never came to Holiday's side unless he needed something; they also claim he was out with a woman the night of her death.

William Dufty was one of McKay's adversaries. While he had no rights to Holiday's estate, he did own the rights to *Lady Sings the Blues*. As one of Holiday's closest friends at the end of her life, he felt it was his duty to get her story made into a movie. On a few occasions the script was optioned, but it was not until 1972 that something materialized. The film *Lady Sings the Blues* starred Diana Ross—who at the time was a former member of the Supremes and a rising solo music star—was highly criticized by those close to Holiday for not maintaining accuracy. (Supposedly the first draft of the script was so truthful about Holiday's life that the producers believed it was unsellable, so parts were changed and sections were exaggerated.) Many close to Holiday had refused to allow

DID YOU KNOW?

BILLIE AND HER GODCHILDREN

It has been argued that in some ways Billie Holiday never mentally matured past nine years old, the age when she dropped out of school and first started showing signs of wanting to live the fast life. In many ways Holiday was just a child, right until her death. But though she could act like a child, she was very much an adult with yearnings for a family. She often spoke of wanting to have children, and she dreamed of retiring to a farm where she could raise a horde of natural and adopted children.

The facts are never very clear, but on multiple occasions, friends of Holiday's have mentioned that she told them she could not have children. Whatever the case there is no record of her being pregnant except for a story about her trying to perform an abortion by sitting in a tub of mustard and water. This story was told to Dufty, her ghostwriter, and as it has not been proven, it is difficult to verify any truth in the statements she gave him.

In lieu of children Holiday doted on the children of friends. Louis McKay had two children from a previous relationship, and according to witness accounts, she treated them well when they were visiting. Many of her friends recognized her desire to be a mother and asked Holiday to be the godmother to their children. She took the role very seriously. She was godmother to the children of Leonard Feather, Mike Gould, Dorothy Winston, Rosemary Clooney, and William Dufty. Clooney quoted Holiday as saying to her when pregnant with her second child, "I think you've got a girl child in your belly this time. And I think I should be her godmother, because it takes a very bad woman to be a good godmother."

In *Lady Sings the Blues* (1972), a film directed by Sidney J. Furie, recording star Diana Ross played the legendary Billie Holiday. The film earned numerous Academy Award nominations, including one for Ross in the category of Best Actress in a Leading Role.

their names to be used. But like Holiday's experience with *New Orleans*, Ross's performance was praised and she won an Academy Award for her work.

A number of novels, biographies, and poems have appeared about Billie Holiday since her death, including "The Day Lady Died," a poem written by American poet Frank O'Hara while he was traveling on a ferry to Staten Island, New York, on the day of her death. Others have paid tribute to Holiday as well. U2 wrote a song, "Angel of Harlem," about her; the United States Postal Service issued a stamp with her image in 1994; and many artists—among them, Nina Simone, Tori Amos, UB40, Diana Ross, Cassandra Wilson, Sting, Jeff Buckley, and Lou Rawls—have covered her signature songs, including the indelible "Strange Fruit."

More than a half-century after Billie Holiday's death, her influence lives on. Her talent, her beauty, and her tragic story have enthralled millions. The fame and appreciation that Holiday so desperately sought during her lifetime would come tenfold after her death. As the events of her difficult life fade into history, the woman and her music have remained.

1946 *Billie Holiday*

1947 *Billie Holiday–Teddy Wilson*; *A Hot Jazz Classic Set, Vol. 1*

1949 *Teddy Wilson and His Orchestra Featuring Billie Holiday*

1950 *An Evening with Eddie Heywood and Billie Holiday*;
Billie Holiday Volume One; *Billie Holiday Volume Two*

1951 *Lover Man*

1952 *Billie Holiday Sings*

1954 *Billie Holiday and Teddy Wilson Orchestras*; *Lady Day*

1956 *The Lady Sings*; *Lady Sings the Blues*; *Carnegie Hall
Concert* (released 1961)

1957 *Ella Fitzgerald & Billie Holiday at Newport*; *A Midsummer
Night's Jazz at Stratford '57* (released 1999); *Sound of Jazz*

1958 *Lady in Satin*; *The Blues Are Brewin'*; *Lover Man*

1915 Born Eleanora Fagan on April 7 in Philadelphia, Pennsylvania. Moves with mother, Sadie Fagan, soon after her birth to Baltimore, where they live near the rest of the Fagan family.

1920 Sadie marries longshoreman Philip Gough on October 20.

1922–1927 Gough abandons Sadie and Eleanora with no explanation. Eleanora is sent to the House of Good Shepherd for Colored Girls on January 5, 1925. In October 1925, Eleanora is released into her mother's custody, and they move to the Fell's Point neighborhood of east Baltimore. Eleanora develops a penchant for the fast life and spends much of her time in a brothel run by Ethel Moore and begins to sing in small clubs for pocket change. In 1926, she is raped by a family acquaintance and is sent back to the House of Good Shepherd. She is released on February 27, 1927, and immediately begins planning to leave for New York City, where Sadie has been working as a maid for a wealthy white family. Arrives in New York later that year.

1929 Arrested, alongside her mother, for solicitation and spends six months incarcerated at Welfare Island.

1930–1932 Begins to sing in clubs and speakeasies to earn money. Has a yearlong engagement at the Nest. Takes the name Billie Halliday, changing the last name from her father's ever so slightly so as not to cash in on his fame.

1933 Hired by Monette Moore to sing at Monette's Supper Club, but the engagement only lasts three weeks. Each night, however, John Hammond is in attendance; he is impressed with her abilities and sets up her first recording date, on November 27, when she performs "Your Mother's Son-in-Law" with Benny Goodman's band. She records another tune, "Riffing the Scotch," on December 18. She earned $35 for each recording. That same year she becomes engaged to her piano accompanist Bobby Henderson.

1934 Moves to the Hot-Cha Bar on Seventh Avenue, and her local fame continues to grow. In November, she is asked to perform at the Apollo Theater. Though their engagement had ended, Billie and Henderson still perform together, including the date at the Apollo.

1935 Begins to record with Teddy Wilson, and these multiple sessions will be considered some of the greatest of her career, as well as some of the greatest in jazz history. She changes her last name to Holiday, and midway through the year, returns to the Apollo and produces one of the most memorable performances of her career. Holiday meets Joe Glaser, who becomes her agent for the rest of her life.

1937 Meets saxophone player Lester Young at a recording session in January, and the two become the closest of friends. He nicknames her "Lady Day," and she in turn dubs him "The President," or "The Prez." On March 1, Holiday receives word that her father has died, due to complications from pneumonia, while touring in Texas. After a long engagement at the Uptown House, she leaves and goes on tour with the Count Basie Orchestra.

1938 Is subjected to racism while on tour, has conflict with management over her singing style, and is released from the Count Basie Orchestra. Joins another touring ensemble, the all-white Artie Shaw Orchestra. Despite Shaw's efforts to make things easy for her, racism becomes a problem, and by the end of the year, she quits the orchestra.

1939 Begins to perform at Café Society, a new venue in the West Village of New York City. Is given "Strange Fruit" by poet Lewis Allan, and this anti-lynching song becomes one of the most treasured of her repertoire.

1941 Marries Jimmy Monroe, after reuniting with him during a run at his brother's club, the Famous Door. After years of drinking and smoking marijuana, Holiday begins to use harder drugs like opium and heroin. Meanwhile she struggles with punctuality and at times does not show up for gigs, including the first night of her second run at Café Society. Club owner Barney Josephson cancels her contract.

1942   Performs in California and Monroe stays behind, thus ending their marriage. Holiday returns to New York, but soon returns to California for a residency, alongside Lester Young, at Billy Berg's Trouville Club. Around this time she meets trumpeter Joe Guy, who has a heroin habit to match Billie's.

1944   Holiday and Guy put together a 16-piece touring band but end up losing money. She moves from Columbia to Decca Records.

1945   Holiday's mother, Sadie, dies. The touring band is disbanded, and she returns to performing in New York City nightclubs and theaters, including a residency at the Down Beat Club.

1946   Performs her first solo concert, at Town Hall, to much acclaim. Later that year Holiday is cast to play a maid in the film *New Orleans*. It is panned and criticized by some for its blatant racism and stereotypical portrayal of African Americans, but she gets the opportunity to work alongside her childhood idol, Louis Armstrong.

1947   Checks herself into a New York clinic to undergo a cure for heroin addiction. The authorities find out about her "cure," and upon her release, she is watched closely. In May her hotel room in Philadelphia is raided, and heroin is found. She escapes arrest but later turns herself in to the police. She is sentenced to a year and a day for narcotics possession and sent to the Federal Reformatory for Women at Alderson, West Virginia.

1948   Released after nine and a half months. There is a welcome-home concert for Holiday at Carnegie Hall, but her ability to perform in New York City is now greatly limited after losing her cabaret card. Despite these restrictions, club owner John Levy is able to circumvent the law and have Holiday perform at his Ebony Club. Levy and she soon become a couple.

1948–1949 Holiday and Levy are arrested for assaulting Billy Berg club patrons on New Year's Eve. Later in 1949 she is arrested in San Francisco, California, for possession of opium, but the charges are dismissed.

1950 Splits with Levy after he does not follow through with his promise to act as guarantor for the pay of Holiday's band. She moves to California for a three-month residency, where her chauffeur is arrested for possessing heroin packets, which are most likely hers. After a show in Philadelphia, she has a falling-out with Lester Young.

1951 Moves to Aladdin Records, for one year, after Decca does not offer her a new contract. Holiday meets Louis McKay who becomes her personal manager, adviser, and soon her husband.

1952 Signs with the Mercury label, run by Norman Granz. Toward the end of the year, she performs on the television broadcast *25th Anniversary in the Music Business* at Carnegie Hall, which celebrates the life of Duke Ellington.

1953 Participates in a television broadcast, *The Comeback Story*, about her life.

1954 Tours Europe, as the headliner, with "Jazz Club U.S.A." Upon her return she performs at the inaugural Newport Jazz Festival and is joined onstage by Lester Young. It is the first time they have seen each other in three and a half years.

1956 Arrested again for narcotics possession in Philadelphia, though the case is later dismissed. Her autobiography, *Lady Sings the Blues*, is published (ghostwritten by William Dufty), and Holiday claims to have never read it.

1957 Moves to Columbia Records, and her relationship with McKay ends.

1958 Lives alone in an apartment near Central Park, and her addiction and mood swings have left her ostracized from many of her friends. She continues to perform but struggles with punctuality. In October she performs at the Monterey Jazz Festival. In the fall Holiday returns to Europe for a short tour through Italy and France.

1959 Becomes quite ill and is diagnosed with problems associated with alcoholism and drug abuse. At her forty-fourth birthday party, her condition has worsened and many of her friends try to force her to go to the hospital. She refuses and is able to perform the following week, in Boston, at the Storyville Club. Her final show is at the Phoenix Theater, in Greenwich Village, and she needs to be escorted home. On May 31, Holiday falls into a coma and is taken to the hospital. On June 12, the police raid her room and find a packet of heroin, but according to her friends she was not using drugs at the end of her life and they believe the drug was either planted or left by a concerned friend who thought it might help comfort her in her final days. On July 17, at 3:10 A.M., Billie Holiday dies.

Blackburn, Julia. *With Billie: A New Look at the Unforgettable Lady Day*. New York: Pantheon, 2005.

Chilton, John. *Billie's Blues: The Billie Holiday Story 1933–1959*. New York: Da Capo Press, 1975.

Clarke, Donald. *Billie Holiday: Wishing on the Moon*. New York: Da Capo Press, 2000.

Davis, Angela Y. *Blues Legacies and Black Feminism: Gertrude "Ma" Rainey, Bessie Smith, and Billie Holiday*. New York: Vintage, 1998.

Gourse, Leslie. *The Billie Holiday Companion: Seven Decades of Commentary*. New York: Schirmer, 1997.

Griffin, Farah Jasmine. *If You Can't Be Free, Be a Mystery: In Search of Billie Holiday*. New York: Random House, 2001.

Holiday, Billie, with William Dufty. *Lady Sings the Blues*. New York: Penguin Books, 1956.

Ingham, Chris. *Billie Holiday*. New York: Welcome Rain Publishers, 2000.

Margolick, David. *Strange Fruit: Billie Holiday, Café Society, and an Early Cry for Civil Rights*. Philadelphia: Running Press, 2000.

Nicholson, Stuart. *Billie Holiday*. Boston: Northeastern University Press, 1997.

O'Meally, Robert. *Lady Day: The Many Faces of Billie Holiday*. New York: De Capo, 1991.

WEB SITES
Billie Holiday: The Official Site of Lady Day
http://www.cmgww.com/music/holiday/

A History of Jazz
http://www.historyjazz.com/

Last.fm: Billie Holiday
http://www.last.fm/music/Billie+Holiday

The Unofficial Billie Holiday Website
http://www.ladyday.net/

page

4: Michael Ochs Archives/Getty Images
9: © Underwood & Underwood/CORBIS
16: © Bettmann/CORBIS
19: Frank Driggs Collection/Getty Archives
26: Frank Driggs Collection/Archive Photos/Getty Archives
29: Frank Driggs Collection/Archive Photos/Getty Archives
36: Metronome/Archive Photos/Getty Images
41: Metronome/Archive Photos/Getty Images
47: Frank Driggs Collection/Archive Photos/Getty Archives
50: Michael Ochs Archives/Getty Images
62: Michael Ochs Archives/Getty Images
66: William Gottlieb/Redferns/Getty Images
73: Charles Hewitt/Picture Post/Hulton Archive/Getty Images
79: GAB Archive/Redferns/Getty Images
80: CBS/Landov
86: Paul Hoeffler/Redferns/Getty Images
89: Paramount Pictures/Photofest

Page numbers in *italics* indicate photos or illustrations.

About the Author

Forrest Cole is a poet and essayist with an MFA from the International Studies Program at the University of Nevada, Las Vegas. He has been a freelance writer for the past 10 years. In his spare time, he is also the owner and chef of a taqueria in Brooklyn, New York.